The Jewish Idea of Culture

The Jewish Idea of Culture

by

Sol Roth

Foreword by

Elie Wiesel

KTAV Publishing House, Inc.
Hoboken, NJ

Library of Congress Cataloging-in-Publication Data

Roth, Sol.
    The Jewish idea of culture / by Sol Roth.
      p.   cm.
    Includes bibliographic references.
    ISBN 0–88125–543–2
    1. Judaism and science. 2. Orthodox Judaism. 3. Jewish law. 4. Jews—
Civilization. I. Title.
BM538.S3R69 1996
296.3'87—dc20   96-252
                                                CIP

Manufactured in the United States of America
KTAV Publishing House, 900 Jefferson Street, Hoboken NJ, 07030

To

Steven and Karen
Sharon
Erica Lynn
Joshua Joseph

Contents

Foreword

What an intriguing title! What does "The Jewish idea of culture" really mean? That there is some opposition between Jewish ideas and culture? Aren't ideas themselves an intrinsic part of culture, be it Jewish or general? Naturally, the term and concept of "culture" are used here in a broad sense.

What the intelligent reader will like in this stimulating and enriching work is the rigor of the author's questioning and the elegance of his desire not to leave questions unexplored. For him nothing can remain obscure. Our predecessors understood things that we still do not know. It is up to us to ask them for help.

A great Hasidic Master once remarked that "for the believer there are no questions and for the non-believer there are no answers." This wise saying does not apply easily to our generation. Today the search for God by the one and the denial of transcendence by the other are less sharply defined and both see incomplete. Almost everywhere one can meet renowned secular scientists who admit their thirst for religiosity, and fervent believers who find in their own faith arguments to question it.

How do we reconcile faith and reason, science and tradition, religious observance and cultural environment? What are the limits beyond which the believer may not go without jeopardizing his faith by violating the Law handed down by Moses and interpreted by our sages? What is the intellectual's place in a society governed by these Masters of Halakha? What is the role of art and the artist in today's changing world?

In his new volume, Rabbi Sol Roth examines these questions which have for centuries preoccupied man open if not to doubt, then at least to philosophical inquiry. I hope it will be read by all who are fascinated by the great and grandiose adventure that the history of Jewish religious thought represents.

A highly respected spiritual leader (of Fifth Avenue Synagogue), erudite thinker and professor of Jewish philosophy at Yeshiva University, Rabbi Roth has already authored several remarkable works on subjects not far removed from this one.

His style is vigorous and his writing clear. One can only marvel at the way in which he introduces into the discussion seekers and teachers such as the Rambam, the Ramban, the revered Harav Kook, the celebrated Rabbi Samson Raphael Hirsch and the incomparable Rabbi Yoshe Ber Soloveitchik.

Through the centuries these luminous minds have explored the issues that the Orthodox Jew, confronted with the cult and the culture of modernity, is often compelled to address. The ambiguous component of destiny in free-will, values and politics, religion and social order—the author deals with these nontemporal themes in a contemporary context.

What is the difference between Torah u'Maada and Torah im Derekh Eretz? In both cases it is the Torah that takes precedence. The Torah is the beginning and the end of all intellectual and spiritual endeavors.

But is it necessary to isolate oneself, to withdraw from the community so as to be able to follow the path of our ancestors, or in other words: must we look for the answer in asceticism, in self-sacrifice?

Granted, the Torah emphasizes the affirmation of life and the respect for the living. But must one keep the Mitzvot because they are useful to our well-being, or because they originate with God?

The famous French Jewish philosopher Henri Bergson speaks of "the two sources of morality and religion. For the orthodox Jew faithful to his tradition, there is only one source: the Torah. It does not explain life; it is life. At times burning, at other times appeasing, it irrigates all our thoughts and all our activities. Thanks to the Torah, it is given to man to recall in prayer and in study the mysterious origin of his existential walk through life and the anguished goal of his passage on earth.

Elie Wiesel

Preface

The ideals of Torah im Derekh Eretz and Torah uMadda are frequently misunderstood and sometimes misinterpreted. They are perceived as compromises rather than ideals, and this, needless to say, is an unfortunate state of affairs. Compromises are appreciated in the world of politics, economics, and wherever the pragmatic method is the appropriate means for resolving tensions, not in religion. A spiritual personality is expected to conduct his life according to principle. To surrender any part of principle because of the demands and pressures of competing and incompatible claims is to display a lack of courage that disappoints and a failure in commitment that offends. Such an approach will not inspire respect and will not gain adherents in the religious community. It is appropriate therefore to state, at the start, that this volume is not about compromises but about ideals.

It should be added that the principal commitment that informs this volume is an acceptance of halakhah, One may argue about whether culture does or does not fit into the intellectual schema of a halakhic Jew, whether it is something that should be excluded from, or be appropriated into, his perspective. However, even for one who believes that it is halakhically correct and logically mandatory to incorporate culture into a Torah point of view—and this is the position of both Torah im Derekh Eretz and Torah uMadda—this ought to be done in the light and in the context of a commitment to the priority of halakhah.

Torah im Derekh Eretz and Torah uMadda do not assert the equality of each member of these conjunctions. The two doctrines merely affirm the fact that, in the halakhic standpoint, the element of culture, identified alternately as Derekh Eretz and Madda, needs to be embraced in a manner compatible with halakhah and in a way that preserves the integrity of the latter.

A note about the concluding chapter of the book! It is of course relevant to the theme of the volume, but it was introduced at the end primarily because it was originally prepared as an independent essay and was not intended, at the time of its writing, to be incorporated into a volume. In addition, placing it there assured continuity in the sequence of the chapters that constitute the body of this work.

The ideas explored in this volume developed during my association with Yeshiva University and its Rabbi Isaac Elchanan Theological Seminary—first as a student and subsequently as a member of the faculty—over a span of time encompassing decades. My work with the synagogues in which I served as spiritual leader also contributed, and significantly, to the ideas articulated here. This is especially true of Fifth Avenue Synagogue, my current congregation, which strives to exemplify, and in a superior manner, the ideals of Torah and culture. I am grateful to these institutions for providing the ambiance in which the ideas offered in this volume could blossom and the motivation to formulate them and to present them for public consideration.

I am indebted to my teacher, Rabbi Joseph B. Soloveitchik, *zecher tzaddik liverakha* (the memory of the righteous is a blessing), whose life was a paradigm of the ideals to whose analysis this book is devoted and whose writings and lectures provided me with the opportunity to explore intellectually that which his biography and thought embodied. Thanks are due to Jacques and Hannah Schwalbe, both of blessed memory, for encouraging me in a variety of ways, many of them expressing a depth of friendship which I shall always recall with reverence to engage in the study of the writings of Rabbi Samson R. Hirsch. I am grateful to Professor Elie Wiesel with whom I have been associated in my synagogue during the last decade and who has been an endless source of inspiration to me for reading this book and writing the introductory foreword.

Sol Roth

March 1996

Acknowledgments

Chapter 1, *"Torah im Derekh Eretz,"* first appeared in the winter 1989 issue of *Tradition* under the title *"Torah im Derekh Eretz:* An Analysis."

Chapter 3, "The Secular," was published in the spring 1992 issue of *Tradition* under the title "A Halakhic Approach to the Secular."

Chapter 9, "Halakhah and Science," is a somewhat expanded and modified version of "The Halakha as a Theoretical Construction," a chapter in *Of Scholars, Savants, and Their Texts* (New York: Peter Lang, 1989), published in honor of Professor Arthur Hyman and edited by Professor Ruth Link-Salinger.

Chapter 14, "Halakhah and Relevance," is a translation and edited version of *"Ortodoxiut Verelevanziut,"* a paper that appeared in volume 2 of the *Sefer Hayovel* (Jerusalem: Mosad Harav Kook, 1984) in honor of Rabbi Joseph B. Soloveitchik.

Introduction

The question addressed in this volume is how Judaism, as a halakhic system, responds to culture. Its concern is not with issues that arise out of contemporary culture alone. Judaism has had to face similar philosophic tensions in every generation because it has never existed in isolation. It has always been surrounded by, and during long stretches of history found itself in the midst of, cultures and civilizations whose values did not coincide with its own. There has always been a domain, identified in rabbinic tradition as *ḥakhmah*, whose status in the context of Torah needed to be delineated. The culture in the era of Maimonides was not at all similar to that which prevails today. The Aristotelian concepts which he employed in his *Guide to the Perplexed* have little in common with contemporary scientific notions about the elements and processes of the universe. Nor is the nineteenth-century culture confronted by Rabbi Samson R. Hirsch analogous in all its details to that with which we are familiar. Cultures are constantly changing; historical processes are incessantly undergoing development. The question of this volume is universal in scope. While the ideas and concepts discussed here are familiar to us, what is affirmed about the relation of Judaism and culture is applicable to every generation.

The main thesis of this book is that culture possesses positive value and is entitled to the sanction and approbation of the halakhic Jew. The attempt to coalesce Torah and culture has occupied many in modern times. This task has especially been undertaken by those who espouse the doctrines of *Torah im derekh eretz* and *Torah umadda*. A discussion of some elements of these doctrines will constitute a major part of the development of this book's essential thesis. Aspects of the theory of *Torah im derekh eretz* as they were formulated by its author, Rabbi Samson R. Hirsch, will be explored. Elements of Rabbi Joseph B. Soloveitchik's exposition of the *Torah umadda* viewpoint, particularly as it appears in his *The Lonely Man of Faith*, will be studied.[1] It will be our aim to elaborate upon the views of these masters and, in addition, to enhance an understanding of the halakhic approach to culture by clarifying other relevant concepts and ideas.

The thrust of this volume is analysis, not demonstration. The perennial approach of those in the halakhic community who have heretofore been occupied with the ideals of *Torah umadda* and *Torah im derekh eretz* has been to exhibit the justification for adopting these ideals in the light of biblical and rabbinic sources. Their goal was primarily to demonstrate the permissibility, even the desirability, by halakhic criteria, of engaging in the study of the various disciplines that constitute the elements of general culture, and of incorporating them into the curriculum of yeshivot. This approach is crucial, though not quite sufficient because it is essentially defensive in orientation. It is primarily a response to those who would eschew culture altogether. The intent of this volume, however, is to exhibit the subject matter of culture and the concepts used to clarify it as an essential part of the schema of halakhic Judaism and of the religious experience of the Jew.

A variety of questions will be addressed. What do the concepts of *Torah im derekh eretz* and *Torah umadda* mean, and how are the respective relationships of *derekh eretz* and *madda* to Torah to be understood in the context of halakhah? It will be shown that these two ideals are not entirely coincident; indeed, there are substantial differences between them. *Torah im derekh eretz* affirms a unity between Torah and culture which is denied by its counterpart. For the latter, a number of issues arise which are not crucial, perhaps not even relevant, for the former. Among them are: How is "secular" to be understood? What is the relationship of the secular to the sacred? Does Judaism allow the radical separation of the immanent universe of nature from the transnatural realm of the transcendent that is so characteristic of other religions? May concepts that emerge in the study of nature be used to clarify ideas indigenous to that which has its source in the transcendent, i.e., Torah and halakhah?

What significance do ideas associated with the study of nature—scientific and mathematical concepts, for example—have for the halakhic mind?

There are issues that are relevant to both doctrines, to *Torah im derekh eretz* as well as *Torah umadda*. Can the experience of values prominently associated with nature—scientific knowledge and the appreciation of beauty, for example—be regarded as religious? There are also values that man seeks to embody in his life and experience, namely, the sense of dignity and the feeling of self-worth. How are these to be interpreted in the context of the two central approaches to culture?

There are other issues explored in this volume which have relevance to the problem of the relation of culture to halakhah. What components of this relation are exhibited in what is usually regarded as the this-worldly character of Judaism? Political processes and the theory that illuminates them are primarily concerned with the organization of human society. How are these incorporated into the system of halakhah? Moral values can be either theologically based or derived from the human condition and the needs of society. To what extent does the latter enter into a halakhic perspective? The concept of destiny appears essentially to be transcendental in nature. Would Judaism grant this, or would it insist that it relates very much to the here-and-now and is substantially a this-worldly affair?

The discussions in this volume by no means deal with all the issues that emerge out of its central thesis, nor do they explore any one of them exhaustively. The enterprise is too large; many volumes would be required to accomplish it, perhaps even a library. My books that have preceded this one, *Science and Religion*, *The Jewish Idea of Community*, and *Halakhah and Politics: The Jewish Idea of a State*, are all, in effect, attempts at clarifying the relationship of elements of human culture to halakhah. The present work has this advantage, however: the challenge of the central thesis as well as the responses to it are made explicit. There is a conscious attempt to clarify the manner in which elements of culture are integrated into a halakhic view of the universe. The book is consequently a more illuminating response to the question it addresses.

It is my hope that whatever contribution this volume may make to an understanding of *Torah umadda* and *Torah im derekh eretz*, it will spur further study of the subject and, in the process, exhibit what I believe are some of the most important features of Judaism as a religion.

1

Torah Im Derekh Eretz

The ideal of *Torah im derekh eretz*, expounded in its modern sense by Samson R. Hirsch, expresses a philosophy and an attitude. Its meaning is not altogether clear. A logical analysis of its component parts will contribute to its clarification.

Three ideas require explication. The easiest is the notion of *derekh eretz*; more difficult is the idea of Torah; most important, in terms of shedding light on the meaning of the ideal, is the analysis of the meaning of *im*.

I

Derekh eretz is an ambiguous concept. One of its meanings is "labor." The phrase in the Ethics of the Fathers, *Yaffeh torah im derekh eretz*, is taken by the commentators to mean that the study of Torah should be accompanied by labor.[1] A second meaning is "acceptable norms of conduct." The Midrash declares that *derekh eretz* preceded Torah by twenty-six generations.[2] Some commentators explain this assertion to mean that the knowledge of principles of conduct, among which moral principles are included, antedated by this span of time the giving of the Torah. Samson R. Hirsch interprets the same midrash in another way. He takes *derekh eretz* to be identical with culture.[3]

We will assign to *derekh eretz* the last of these meanings and take it as the counterpart of the English word "culture." Of course, the term "culture" is no less ambiguous. We will, however, in conformity with the way it was understood by Samson R. Hirsch, regard it as referring to all the achievements of human civilization. It will include science and technology, ethics and politics, the literary, musical, and plastic arts.

1

II

To delineate the meaning of "Torah" is a task that is considerably more difficult. The word is used in the Torah community in a variety of ways. First and foremost, "Torah" refers to the scroll normally located in the ark. But the word has a more basic connotation. It should be recalled that rabbinic literature distinguishes between the *ketav*, the script, and the *lashon*, the language. The script consists of marks (e.g., the letters that appear on the parchment). The language includes the meanings of these marks. It should be noted that the meanings of the marks in the scroll are not found on the parchment; they are located in the minds of those who understand the Hebrew language. These meanings are also Torah and, no doubt, in a superior sense. One may argue that such meanings are part of the Oral Law (which also includes precepts above and beyond anything that may be inferred from the Written Law), and, since meanings are more significant than script, the Oral Law is to be regarded as Torah in a sense that gives it priority over the Written Law. Clearly the person who embodies the precepts of Torah in his thought and behavior can also be labeled as Torah, and perhaps in an even superior sense. Hence, the judgment of the Talmud, "How foolish are those people who rise for the Torah and fail to rise for a *gavra rabba*, (a great Torah personality)."[4]

The word "Torah," however, may refer to other things as well. We speak of a Torah institution, a designation which may be appropriately applied to a yeshiva in which Torah is studied, a synagogue in which Torah scrolls are housed and read, and even a mikveh, which, while it does not normally contain a Torah scroll, provides the means of fulfilling many of the mitzvot of Torah. In fact, any object which is used for the purpose of performing a mitzvah may be identified, for that reason, as a Torah object. Items such as a sukkah, an etrog, a tallit, a shofar, and so on, come under the rubric of Torah in this sense.

One may expand the meaning of Torah and argue that even objects which are not essential for the purpose of fulfilling a mitzvah but simply enhance the beauty of the mitzvah might be included in the category of Torah. The Talmud, accordingly, teaches *hitnaeh lefa-nav b'mitzvot*, "introduce a dimension of beauty in the performance of mitzvot."[5] One can satisfy the requirements of the mitzvah of tzitzit with an ugly tallit, but the rabbis urged the use of one that is aesthetically attractive. The element of beauty is, accordingly, brought into the realm of Torah.

This is precisely what Abraham I. Kook intended when he said, *hehadash yitkadesh*, "the new must be sanctified."[6] If a novel object emerges in the course of human experience, it ought not to be rejected; on the contrary, by being brought within the boundaries of Torah, i.e., by being used as a means to perform a mitzvah or to increase its aesthetic appeal, it becomes a Torah object.

III

The most significant of the ideas that require analysis is that sug-gested by the word *im*, which in its literal translation means "with." Several points need to be stressed by way of clarifying the meaning that S. R. Hirsch attaches to this word.

In the first place, "with" is to be understood as the suggestion that *derekh eretz*, i.e., culture, is to be in some sense incorporated into the realm of Torah. It should not be taken to mean that culture and Torah are both legitimate enterprises, and that both ought to be pursued irrespective of the fact that they bear no relation to each other. The latter approach may be no less valid—in fact it is expressed in the analogous ideal entitled *Torah umadda*—but it is not what S. R. Hirsch had in mind. The one who expressed the *Torah umadda* concept in its most striking form is Rabbi Joseph B. Soloveitchik. In a fascinating essay entitled "The Lonely Man of Faith," he distinguished between the two aspects of the human per-sonality. He referred to one as Adam I and the other as Adam II. The biblical mandate given to Adam I is *vekhivshuha*, "conquer the universe." It commands that man shall be active and creative in sci-ence and technology, in social, political, and moral affairs, in the pursuit of aesthetic norms and objects of beauty. The mandate for Adam II, on the other hand, is *l'avda u'leshamra*, "to serve and to

observe." This is the command that man shall submit to God by way
of prayer and observance. The Adam I side of man, accordingly,
prods him to engage in cultural activities; the Adam II aspect
prompts him to involve himself in Torah. The two pursuits are thus
essentially independent of each other, though each has divine sanction.

On this view, culture need not be incorporated into the domain of
Torah; the two are separate and apart. According to S. R. Hirsch, on
the other hand, culture, if it is to be legitimate from the Torah
standpoint, must be brought into some significant relation to Torah.

The relation of culture to Torah in the Hirsch perspective, and this
is the second relevant observation, is twofold. Culture is, first, a
means to Torah, and second, a part of Torah. He writes, "Twenty-six
generations did *derekh eretz* precede Torah. . . . the way is culture,
and only then can one reach to the tree of life, to the Torah. Culture
starts the work of educating the generations of mankind, and the
Torah completes it."[7] Hence culture is a means, a prerequisite, to
the acquisition of Torah. But later in the same passage we read, "For
us Jews, Torah and *derekh eretz* are one."

It should be noted, however, that even when Hirsch speaks of culture as a means, he does not necessarily intend to exclude the possibility that it is also a part of Torah. There are two varieties of means.
A ladder is a means to reach the roof. Once the ladder has been
scaled, it can be discarded. Mathematics is a means to progress in
the science of physics. Even when progress has been made, mathematics is incorporated in the science and becomes part of it. In the
latter instance, the means has become a part. This is the sense in
which Hirsch regards culture as both means and part of Torah.
Obviously, given the exposition above of the various levels of meaning of Torah, it is not at all difficult to regard culture as a part of
Torah as well.

This leads to the third and major point, namely, that the fundamental difference between those who espouse the *Torah im derekh
eretz* philosophy and those who do not is one of attitude. Primarily,
the followers of Hirsch adopt a positive view of human experience in
general; they maintain an openness to the achievements of the

human mind and to cultural progress. They are willing to take the risk that science and philosophy might be perceived, though erroneously, as antagonistic to religion and erode Jewish commitment. They believe, however, that the risk is minimal; that given the open society in which we live, the risk is, in any case, ever present: and that the integration of culture into Torah is a better expression of Torah's attitude toward human life and experience than the bifurcation that results from its exclusion.

The advocates of the Hirschian ideal also adopt the attitude that Torah is not a closed and an excluding system. On the contrary it is open and stands ever ready to incorporate novel components. These additions may be elaborations of principles already recognized as part of Torah, or they may be applications of such principles to new areas of human activity. They may also consist of a variety of cultural achievements which hold promise of enhancing the religious life of the Jew. Those who support the *Torah im derekh eretz* ideal resist the notion that the domain of sanctity is complete and that novel arenas of human experience are forever barred admission.

Ultimately, those who accept the Hirschian ideal adopt a morally monistic view of the universe. Moral dualism presupposes antagonism and opposition. A morally dualistic view of man perceives him as consisting of an evil body and a good soul that are constantly in conflict. A morally dualistic view of the universe regards the material world as hostile to the interests of its spiritual counterpart. It sees the City of God as engaged in a never-ending struggle with the city of man. Such a perspective would inevitably prompt a rejection of that which is judged to be evil and its consignment to a realm that must forever remain removed from that which is sacred and divine. Those who identify with the *Torah im derekh eretz* doctrine, on the other hand, insist on the moral unity of the universe.

Samson R. Hirsch was just such a monist. He argued that the human body ought not to be perceived as evil in view of the fact that it was, according to biblical account, fashioned by God Himself.[8] He insisted that the achievements of Western civilization, as has already been noted, have a place in the fabric of Torah. He maintained that the fruits of Emancipation—freedom and equality—are coherent with Torah commitments.[9] He taught that the accumulation of material goods is a blessing and a divine mandate if they are used for the purpose of realizing God's aims on earth.[10]

IV

Torah im derekh eretz is accordingly a philosophy and a set of attitudes that express a genuine Torah perspective.

2

Torah Umadda: Tension and Resolution

Torah umadda, a motto adopted by many in the Jewish religious community, expresses the view that one ought to be prepared to adopt two noncongruent theoretical schemes of things and to live with both. The two nonconverging points of view are not merely different, they are at times antithetical. It remains for the religious mind to coalesce and integrate them into a harmonious unity. The two schemes are identified alternatively, one as Torah and the other as *madda*, i.e., contemporary culture.

The *Torah umadda* view does not grant that it is at all possible to combine Torah and culture into a single logically coherent discipline. Their fundamental terms cannot be defined in terms of each other, and their basic premises are logically independent of each other. Adherents of this point of view will not even admit that culture, in any of its parts, may be regarded as a component of the large domain of Torah. The two are different in orientation, in direction, and in thrust.

This is the significance of the letter *u* which connects *Torah* to *madda*. If the slogan had been formulated as *Torah im madda*, it would have included in its meaning the idea that Torah and culture are one, either in the sense that a logical unity of both is possible or that culture may be regarded as a component of Torah.[1] The use of the letter *u* suggests that no such unity is assumed.

A metaphor suggested by the science of chemistry may help to illuminate the distinction. Two chemical elements may coexist in a mixture or in combination. Hydrogen and oxygen exist together in the atmosphere in a mixture, but in water in combination. *Torah im*

7

madda asserts a combination of the two; *Torah umadda* declares that the two are together merely in mixture.[2]

Advocates of *Torah umadda*, in effect, declare: We are aware of the fact that in many ways the two are incommensurate; that they do not belong together. We know that some of their elements are radically different, even incompatible. We grant that to appropriate both into a single biography will result in unresolvable tensions for the individual who does so. Notwithstanding, we are convinced that the two can be harmonized, and that this is the true and creative way to live a genuine Torah life.

Indeed, this view is expounded by Rabbi Joseph B. Soloveitchik in his classic "The Lonely Man of Faith."[3] Adam I is the man of culture who is creative in the domain of nature. His aim is to exercise control over nature in the interests of serving himself and in the process mankind as well. He takes initiatives, he solves problems and produces the mechanisms that will improve the quality of human life. Adam II is the man of Torah, essentially and exclusively concerned with submission to God's will through obedience to Torah precept and by involving himself in a direct relationship with God through prayer. The two approaches are clearly different, each having a different direction and thrust, yet both are to be embodied, in varying degrees, in each human personality. The result is, of course, tension and inner struggle. This, however, is the fate of man and the direction that is most productive in human life.

The various tensions in the *Torah umadda* personality will be explored, and the creativity arising out of the process of resolving these tensions will be discussed.

I

Torah umadda expresses polarities and tensions of two varieties—one explicit and secondary, the other implicit and fundamental. Explicitly, it refers to two incommensurate disciplines with which the human mind can occupy itself. One is Torah; the other is culture. They are radically different in that Torah is the fruit of God's mind while culture is the invention of the human mind. Obviously, the two cannot be placed in the same category.

Implicitly, *Torah umadda* directs attention to the problem of self-assertion vis-à-vis self-denial. In the pursuit of cultural achievements, the human being experiences great ego satisfaction.[4] In the pursuit of Torah, an individual exhibits self-denial, i.e., he suppresses his own ego's inclinations in the interests of responding to the will of God.

We may put this in another way. The Torah component in the human personality manifests itself in an attitude that may be identified as covenantal, and the *madda* factor is displayed in an attitude that may be called contractual. The covenantal element is expressed in a commitment that is categorical and unconditional. When an obligation is assumed, as the people of Israel did at Sinai and subsequently in the fields of Moab, by oath and adjuration, it is one-sided and unconditional. It is a commitment to perform without any expectation of reciprocity or reward. It involves a declaration on the part of one who undertakes the commitment that he is prepared to serve. Even more, he perceives service as the primary aim of his existence. The contractual component, on the other hand, leads to conditional commitment, and when it is expressed, there is a demand for mutuality. A person in a contractual posture does not understand giving without receiving in return. He is, in effect, a businessman who seeks a reciprocal commitment from the one with respect to whom he undertakes an obligation and anticipates a profit.[5]

The thrust of an individual in the contractual mode is *self*-assertion. He may become involved in relationships, but even in this state, his concern is essentially personal advantage and self-aggrandizement. A student studying with his teacher, a young man engaged romantically, as distinguished from platonically, with a young woman, a businessman signing a contract with an associate are all involved in relations of the contractual variety; their essential goal is to advance their self-interest. The focus of a person in the covenantal mode is a *relation* which, to him, is of transcending significance. A pious man seeking involvement with the Supreme

Being, friends who are committed to each other on the pattern of the biblical Jonathan and David, a patriotic individual in the process of making the supreme sacrifice for his countrymen are more concerned with enhancing the relationships in which they are involved than with their own personal well-being. These illustrate the covenantal posture.

We may, for the sake of clarification, utilize Martin Buber's classic categorization of two fundamental human attitudes, namely, the I-thou and the I-it relations. When I address another as a thou, i.e., in the second person, I perceive him as no less important than myself, and consequently my relation with him assumes overriding significance. When I perceive him as an it, i.e., in the third person, I assign to him a subordinate status, and I am prepared to utilize him for my own purposes. In these circumstances, it is not the relation that counts but my personal advantage and well-being.

Since both of these attitudes inhere in each individual human being, we are compelled to countenance a doctrine of dualism with respect to man. It is not, however, a moral dualism. We ought not to regard the inclination to self-assertion as an unqualified evil and the tendency to self-denial in the interest of assuring a covenantal relation as an unadulterated good. Both are desirable, indeed, necessary.

The rabbis put it this way. On the verse in the Bible describing God's assessment of His creation, which reads, "And God saw, and behold, it was very good," the rabbis declare, "*It was good* refers to the inclination to do good, and *it was very good* refers to the inclination to do evil, for were it not for the inclination to do evil, men would not build homes, get married, cultivate vineyards," etc.[6] Clearly, the inclination to do evil is not regarded as evil by the rabbis; to the contrary, they identify it as very good. It is merely an inclination, which when misused and misapplied leads to evil, but nevertheless is very good when used for self-assertive activities that are normal and essential to human life and well-being. By moral standards, therefore, both inclinations, though antithetical, are to be designated as good.

There are many illustrations of this point, of which only a few will be cited. Justice and mercy are both moral ideals. Justice, however, is most frequently called upon to support a thrust to self-assertion, while mercy is normally expressed in other-directed activities. When individuals in courts and nations in international forums argue in the name of justice, it is usually to advance a goal or a cause which will serve their interests. In a display of mercy, there is unselfishness and concern for others. There is tension between the two, but it is not the tension that normally prevails between good and evil. And Judaism does not repudiate justice, in all contexts, in favor of mercy.

The halakhah has a principle termed *din* and another designated *lifnim mishurat hadin. Din* requires that in all adjudications the principle of justice be rigorously applied; *lifnim mishurat hadin* demands that in certain specified contexts, a gesture of mercy is more appropriate. A rich man finds something whose owner cannot be identified; *din* allows him to keep it. But if the finder knows for certain that the lost item belongs to an identifiable person who is poor, *lifnim mishurat hadin* declares that he ought to return it.[7] The halakhah, accordingly, allows an individual to exercise his right of self-assertion in one set of circumstances, and demands a selfless gesture in another. The self-asserting and other-regarding postures both have moral sanction.

This conclusion is also implicit in the two concepts of perfection projected in biblical literature. There is the ideal of *sheleimut* and that of *temimut.* The former refers to the perfection of the individual personality and to the cultivation of his abilities and talents. On the verse in the Bible, "And Jacob arrived *shalem* [in a state of perfection] in the city of Shechem," Rashi explains that he arrived perfect in body, perfect, i.e., without loss, in his material possessions and perfect in knowledge.[8] These acquisitions refer to personal attainments, not to the quality of relationships. *Temimut,* on the other hand, refers to perfection in relationships and especially in relations with the Supreme Being. God says to Abraham, "Walk before Me and be perfect (*tamim*)."[9] The perfection referred to here is described in the phrase "Walk before me," which connotes a relationship.

In brief, the contractual attitude is self-regarding; the covenantal is other-directed. An individual must exhibit both in varying circumstances, and both have moral worth. Since neither of these postures is morally reprehensible, the tension experienced by the religious person is not essentially of a moral character. It may become such, but in pursuing both his own well-being in the contractual mode and his selfless commitments to others in the covenantal mode, he does nothing that is morally unacceptable. What, then, is the nature of the tension experienced by the religiously oriented individual?

II

The tension is essentially spiritual in character. While acts of self-assertion are morally acceptable, the man of religious commitments who associates infinity with the Divine Being, and perceives the religious obligations imposed upon him as expressing an equally infinite demand, finds it difficult to understand how the finite claims upon him that flow from his contractual nature can be assigned any temporal or spatial domain in which they might be legitimately expressed. What validity can finite inclinations have when confronted by infinite demands made by the Infinite Being?

This is the paramount problem for the religious mind. It is precisely this state of affairs that often leads to extremism. The internal dynamic of the religious mind prompts the maximal religious involvement, and this may very well lead to the adoption of immoderate religious positions. An individual of such a bent is incapable of dealing with tension, especially when it involves a confrontation between an infinite demand and a finite one. The simple response is to immerse oneself completely in the infinite. This, however, is not the creative approach; it is not the approach that is consistent with the *Torah umadda* point of view.

The inner struggle described here may be resolved in either of two ways. One may opt in favor of the *Torah im derekh eretz* view, which claims that there is in reality no tension at all. *Derekh eretz*, i.e., the cultural pursuit, is regarded as part of Torah and is perceived by the individual who engages in it as an expression of the pure and unadulterated religious impulse that brings him directly into relation with the Divine Being. This view is also, at least to an extent, maintained by S. D. Luzzatto, who argues that when a religious person has reached the level of *kedushah*, sanctity, he engages in what might otherwise be regarded as contractual activities for covenantal reasons; i.e., he eats, clothes himself, and generally takes care of his needs, not for his own sake but for the sake of God.[10]

The *Torah umadda* approach, on the other hand, affirms the existence of the tension. It argues, however, that the adoption of the contractual posture is itself a response to the Infinite Will. Rabbi Soloveitchik put it this way. One of the commands God gave to Adam I is *vekhivshuha*, which means "and conquer the world." Man, on this view, is obligated to immerse himself in the world of nature and culture in order to exercise control over it, to exploit it, to utilize it in his own interests, and to enhance the quality of human life.[11] In this mode, man does not experience his immersion in the natural world as religious, but as a human enterprise with divine sanction.

In responding to specifically prescribed Torah precepts, an individual is aware that, in doing what the halakhah requires, he is involved directly in a relationship with God. It is, metaphorically speaking, the relation of a father and a child, a sovereign and a subject, a master and a servant. The awareness of being a child, subject, and servant in relation to a Father, Sovereign, and Master is essential to the religious posture. No such awareness is present when an individual pursues his own interests or does that which is advantageous to the community by means of actions that flow from the contractual mode of his existence. There is an awareness of God as the One who endorses and encourages, even requires, such activity, but in this context, God is experienced as present in the background, much as a father stands removed from his child's perception in order to encourage the child to act according to his own assessment as to what is in his best interests. The child's behavior is then guided by impulse, inclination, even reason, and he receives no interference until the parent sees him violating some cardinal rule of discipline that has been communicated to him. Having circumscribed the domain of permissible behavior by parameters of a moral and spiritual nature, man too is left to his own calculations, is granted a domain of freedom and allowed any conduct so long as it is not disparate with the rules emanating from the Divine Will, to which man is obligated to respond.

This is one aspect of the meaning of freedom of the will, according to its Jewish conception. A human being is not merely granted the power to do good or evil (and this the usual meaning assigned to freedom of the will); he is also granted the right to do as he wills in a large domain so long as he refrains from violating divine imperatives. This indeed is the meaning of the biblical declaration, "Thou shalt proclaim liberty throughout the land to all the inhabitants thereof," on which Rashi comments, "As one who lives in an inn; he lives wherever he wants to."[12] There is a realm of freedom in which a person may behave as he sees fit. A human being conducting himself according to egoistic utilitarian considerations, when these are not in conflict with the Divine Will, cannot therefore be regarded as disrespectful, disobedient, and recalcitrant with respect to the Divine Being—certainly not on the Jewish view. To the contrary, as Rabbi Soloveitchik declares, he is fulfilling a divine mandate.

Asceticism receives no sanction in the halakhah. A Jew is not allowed to isolate himself from society, enclose himself in a hermitage, and deprive himself of those satisfactions that bring fulfillment to normal human impulses. Even when a Nazirite denies himself the pleasures of wine for a limited period of time, he is regarded, by some of the sages, as a sinner.[13] There are two reasons for the halakhic objection to asceticism. One is to prevent an individual from renouncing his obligations to society. An ascetic, living as a hermit, cannot make a contribution to the well-being of his fellow men, for he denies himself the opportunity to be involved in social concerns and to respond to the pressing issues of the day. The other is to assure a normal life for contractual man by acceptable human standards.

Man was created with an ego, a self. An ego includes a bundle of impulses that are translated into human interests that crave satisfaction. The halakhah demands that an individual restrain the goadings and proddings of his ego in the interests of obedience to the Divine Will; it does not require its obliteration. In a sense, ego satisfactions are always present for man in both his contractual and his covenantal posture. In the contractual mode, the pleasures and joys that he experiences are independent of any satisfactions that he might have made available to others. In that state, his sole preoccupation is his own personal fulfillment. In the covenantal mode, his joys and satisfactions are a function of his relationships. If, through his conduct, he is able to enhance his relations to an other—be it the Divine Other or even a human other—he experiences a sense of well-being. This is expressed, for example, in the halakhic concept of *simhah shel mitzvah*, the joy of fulfilling commandments. Such joy, though it derives from an awareness of involvement and relation with the Divine Being, also brings personal satisfaction, i.e., ego fulfillment. This is manifest, as well, in the ecstasy of the martyr. In the moment when an enthusiastically committed religious individual makes the supreme sacrifice, he experiences unique and indescribable joy, which results in extraordinary ego fulfillment. What distinguishes the joy of ecstasy, a covenantal sentiment, from the pleasure of eating, a contractual feeling, for example, is that the latter is based on gratifications enjoyed by the subject insofar as he exists in isolation, while the former finds joy far more intense in relation.

It should be added that the enterprise of immersing oneself in the world of culture is far less difficult for the *Torah im derekh eretz* personality than it is for the advocate of *Torah umadda*. The former perceives even his cultural involvements as embodying relations with God and, therefore, constituent of his religious experience; while the latter, in the course of his cultural pursuits, sees himself as, at least temporarily, removed from a direct relation with the Divine Being. Given that the genuinely religious person seeks to maximize his involvement with God, the contractual posture, even while he understands it to be divinely mandated, is a difficult one for him to adopt.

III

How then can the tension that plagues the religious individual because of the contradiction between the contractual and covenantal components in his personality be resolved? It will not do merely to say that both have legitimacy and are entitled to expression. Both make identical claims on the time and energy of the human being, who in the process of acting in the contractual mode, necessarily excludes the covenantal attitude from engaging his attention. It is not possible to move in two opposite directions at the same time; nor is it possible to exemplify both the covenantal and the contractual posture in the same action simultaneously. This state of affairs is compounded, as has been noted, by the circumstance that the religious individual seeks to maximize the religious component of his total experience.

We must elaborate on a point alluded to before. A human being can become involved with the Divine Being in two ways. In one, he embodies, in his actions, the *tzelem elohim*, the image of God; in the other, his actions bring him into direct relation with God. To embody the image of God is to behave as He does, i.e., creatively, in the domain of nature and society. There is no requirement, in this posture, to be totally unselfish but only to be creative. It may be assumed that, in the process of being truly creative for himself, he does that which will be advantageous to others as well. When he behaves in an unselfish manner in relation to others without any intent of securing some benefit for himself, then if he is doing so out of commitment to halakhic precept, he is accordingly acting in a manner that brings him into direct relation with God. The latter does not require creativity but merely submission.

Rabbi Soloveitchik puts it this way. The conduct of Adam I manifests the *tzelem elohim*; he is accordingly a creative personality.[14] He is inventive, not only in the realm of theoretical science and technology, but also in the domain of values—moral and aesthetic—in which he applies utilitarian criteria.[15] Adam II, who is directly involved in a relation with God, on the other hand, seeks redemption in defeat, i.e., utter submission to God's will.[16]

The resolution of the problem is now at hand. The religiously minded individual seeks to maximize his involvement with God, but he is not frustrated in activities that reflect his contractual nature when he realizes that, even in this framework, he still embodies God's image. He is aware of the fact that even when expressing his creative urge, he is not entirely removed from the Divine Being. Even more, he knows that it is precisely the presence of the image of God within himself that guarantees the possibility of his creativity. This knowledge, consequently, has a moderating effect on his ego. Since it is the divine element in man that issues in creativity, he cannot by himself take full credit for his accomplishments. There is a Senior Partner to whom he must be forever grateful.

But there are other considerations that contribute to the resolution of this tension. In the first place, the priorities in this state of affairs compel the conclusion that behavior that expresses the image of God is subordinate to that through which the individual experiences a direct relation to God. If A is prior to B, A is not ignored in the process of pursuing B; to the contrary, B must, to some extent, conform to the requirements of A even while A does not engage conscious attention. One may suppose that even scientists would grant that moral considerations take precedence over the acquisition of truth. Many men of science hesitated over the development of atomic power because of its potential to destroy mankind. The subordination of science to morality means that science must conform to the requirements imposed on it by morality. Analogously, a human being in the *madda* posture is prevented from doing anything that may constitute a violation of a Torah precept because of the priority of Torah.

IV

Tension is itself creative, and this holds true for the tension that is characteristic of the person who is committed to *Torah umadda*. There is one obvious form of creativity which is not related to the tension, namely, the creativity that is rooted in the fact that he bears the *tzelem elohim* and which is manifested in the realm of nature and culture. The other form derives from the tension itself and that results in creativity in the realm of the spirit.

The religious personality, as stated above, is pulled in two opposite directions, both of which include involvement with the Divine Being. He seeks simultaneously, on the one hand, a direct relation with God, i.e., to be in His presence, and, on the other, to exhibit the image of God in his actions. Whenever he finds himself in one state, he remains aware of the need to move to the other. When in direct relation to God in prayer and the observance of mitzvot, he is conscious of his obligation to immerse himself creatively in the world of human affairs, and when engaged in the latter, he is guided at every moment by halakhic guidelines and by the need to ensure that all he does will not violate but, to the contrary, will enhance the life of Torah. This state of affairs is the basis for creativity of a spiritual variety.

To combine Torah with *madda* is by no means easy. It involves tension, restlessness, struggle; but also creativity of a natural, cultural, and spiritual variety. Indeed, from the Torah standpoint, this is the inevitable fate and the destiny of the halakhic Jew.

3

The Secular

Halakhah adopts a positive and constructive attitude toward things secular. Such objects are not to be repudiated on the grounds that the ideal of the religious experience requires the exclusion of everything from human awareness and activity except that which is sacred. Indeed, this is neither possible nor desirable. It is important, therefore, to indicate the place of the secular in the perspective of the sacred, i.e., to describe the halakhic approach to the secular.

At the outset, a distinction should be made between the secular and the profane. These two realms are not the same, though the terms denoting them are frequently used interchangeably. Here the word "profane" will be taken to refer to objects (e.g., idols) and events (e.g., an act of idolatry or adultery) which are incompatible with halakhic standards of sanctity; while the term "secular" will be understood as referring to things that are essentially neutral by halakhic criteria and which may assume a sacred or profane character, in the context of human behavior, depending on how they are utilized.

The *Torah umadda* approach insists on a distinction between the secular and the profane. The halakhah divides the domain of existence into a number of categories which reflect a declining order of religious status. The following is a nonexhaustive sampling of these classifications. The realm of *kodesh*, the sacred, contains that which is on the highest level of religious worth. Below it is that which is denoted by *ḥol*, the secular. Somewhere on the scale, perhaps beneath the secular, is the classification of *tamei*, the spiritually impure, and, at the bottom is the *toeivah*, or abomination. This last may be included in the category of the profane. The *ḥol* can be sanctified, the *tamei* can, in many instances, be purified, but the *toeivah* is inherently contradictory to Judaism's fundamental commitments and is consequently profane.

The Torah umadda view is not willing to lump all nonsacred things into the one category of the profane; it recognizes important differences between the profane and the secular. It holds that while the former must be unequivocally rejected, a positive attitude may be adopted toward the latter. The profane is incompatible with halakhah and consequently cannot coexist with it; the secular, on the other hand, depending on its relationships, may be entirely consistent with halakhah, and so long as this is the case, is welcomed into the domain of positive Jewish experiences.

I

In order to exhibit the meaning of the secular and the halakhic attitude toward it, we now turn to the primary task, namely, to make clear the difference between the sacred and the secular, between kodesh and hol, and to exhibit the relationship between them. The first point to be stressed is that the sacred requires service, while the secular calls for creativity.

There is a difference in the biblical meanings of the words melakhah and avodah. Both of these Hebrew terms are usually translated as "work," but at bottom they are fundamentally dissimilar. melakhah refers to creative activity in nature—the thirty-nine categories of work that are prohibited on the Sabbath because of their creative character are called melakhah—while avodah refers to work, not of creation, but of service. Indeed, this word is related to eved, which means "servant" or "slave." The essence of melakhah is revealed in, for example, the planting and harvesting of a crop or the construction of an edifice; the essence of avodah is manifest in that which a parent does for a child or in the responses of a pious Jew to the will of God.

Avodah depends, first of all, on a self-transcending purpose. Where there is a master or a loved one toward whom or for whose sake one is undertaking an activity, there is the possibility of service. The source of inspiration for such actions may even be an ideal, in which case we speak of service to a cause. When one's labor is not directed toward something external to and higher than oneself, when a man is himself the sole object of his efforts, what he does is not in the category of *avodah*.

Melakhah, on the other hand, does not require self-transcendence. One who engages in it is concerned essentially with personal creativity. And even where another for whom work is being done exists, as, for example, in the case of employer and employee, the goal of a man's activity in relation to his labor or to his employer is essentially advancing his own self-interest.

Further, the standard by which we judge *melakhah* is degree of creativity. The task need not be difficult; it need not require the expenditure of an enormous amount of effort; it is praiseworthy to an extent proportional to its creativity. *Avodah*, on the other hand, is assessed, not by what is accomplished, but by the amount of laborious and painful activity that an individual undertakes on behalf of another.

In any case, what is crucial in service, or, if you will, in a labor of love, is an awareness of an other in whose behalf or for whose sake an activity is undertaken. If there is no consciousness of another person or a cause or the Divine Being, then no matter how difficult the labor and oppressive the work, it is not *avodah*. Maimonides speaks of prayer as *avodah shebalev*, a service of the heart.[1] If it is *avodah*, it is self-transcending. The implication is that we engage in prayer, even when we utter petitions, not to acquire something for ourselves, but to exhibit our dependence on the Almighty. And even if one is serving under coercion, the awareness of a master is crucial to the identification of that which he is doing as service.

The decision as to whether an action belongs to the domain of the secular or the sacred depends, therefore, on whether it is accompanied by an awareness that we are responding to the Almighty, or whether it is associated with the consciousness of an object which is prompting our creative attention. *melakhah* is work in the secular domain. In a secular act, one is normally preoccupied with the object that engages his attention. It is not, essentially, an encounter in a self-transcending experience with the Divine Being. When, however, an act is accompanied by a conscious awareness of God and an intention to fulfill His commands, i.e., to serve, it is one which is inspired by a self-transcending purpose and is, accordingly, in the category of the sacred.

It is interesting to note that there are times when *melakhah*, the creative act, and *avodah*, the act of service, come together. When a scribe is writing a Sefer Torah, a scroll of the Law, his task involves both creativity and service. It is for this reason that he must consciously declare, prior to undertaking the writing of the scroll and immediately before he writes a name of the Divine Being, that what he is doing is for the sake of God's Holy Name.[2] (Interestingly, the requirement is that the act be preceded by a declaration of intention, but the intent need not be kept in mind during the performance of the act. In the creative process, one's thoughts must be totally preoccupied with whatever one is seeking to accomplish.)

Awareness of a transcendent Other toward whom his labor is directed is what turns what a man does into an act of *avodah* and brings it into the domain of sanctity. If what he is doing is essentially creative, and accordingly belongs in the realm of *melakhah*, the introductory thought that it is being done for the sake of God translates it into a simultaneous act of *avodah*. Indeed, this is an essential element in the process of sanctifying the secular.

II

A second distinction between the sacred and the secular, and this one flows from the first, is that the values emanating from the domain of the sacred are transcendent and imposed on the human being from without, while those deriving from the realm of the secular are immanent, i.e., they emerge out of the human condition. Such values are normally adopted for aesthetic and utilitarian reasons. The view which recognizes the legitimacy of the secular, therefore, grants that values derived from a source independent of the sacred can also be normative.

Clearly, nontranscendent and, consequently, secular values are recognized as legitimate in halakhah. There is an array of aesthetic norms that are required by halakhah but which are not its central focus. We are instructed in a general way *hitna'eh lefanav bamitzvot*, "introduce beauty into the performance of halakhic precepts,"[3] but the canons of beauty to which we are to adhere in such conduct are not enunciated. We are to use an adorned tallit, a decorated sukkah, tefillin that are appealing to the eye, but how these objects are to be shaped and fashioned to satisfy the requirement of beauty is not revealed. Aesthetic values are taken as expressions of a sense of appreciation that is fundamentally human. What is required is that values rooted in human nature shall be associated with the fulfillment of precepts with a transcendental source in order that the religious experience shall be enhanced by the sense of the pleasant. In any case, aesthetic values are basically secular in character.

The sovereign in Jewish life was obligated to concern himself with the task of *tikkun haolam*, the improvement of society. He was expected, among other things, to introduce legislation, as circumstances demanded, to assure the viability and progress of the communal life of the Jewish people. His enactments, in general, were not to contradict the halakhah, but were supplementary to it. He was not required, as was the case with the shofet, or judge, to concern himself with bringing to mankind the *inyan elohi*, the divine, i.e., the transcendental, element.[4] The laws that he introduced invariably found their basis in some need of human society. They emerged out of the human condition and were accordingly secular. Justice, for example is a transcendental principle, but legislation such as social security to spare the aged the suffering that accompanies starvation is a sovereign and therefore secular enactment. Charity is biblically prescribed and mandated by a transcendental source; legislation that creates social institutions to aid the poor is a human invention.

The conclusion that many social norms are secular in character also follows from the halakhic validation of cultural relativity. It is not the case that every society in every temporal period guides itself by identical norms. Variations in cultural conditions are often reflected in differing systems of social-political values. A capitalist democracy and one guided by the principles of economic socialism are equally acceptable forms of government, according to the halakhah, so long as each embodies the principle of justice. Nevertheless, each exemplifies a different economic and political value system. Since both are sanctioned, and neither is transcendentally prescribed, it follows that each reflects the human condition in a different cultural context and each is an expression of human and, consequently, secular values.

Even ethical principles may, in some instances, have a secular character. The issue has received extensive discussion in Jewish moral philosophy. It is generally recognized that the explicitly articulated precepts of the Law do not suffice to exhaust all the ethical imperatives that are to guide human conduct. Nachmanides, in his commentary on the Bible, makes this point explicit. He writes:

> It is impossible to enumerate in the Torah all the precepts required to guide the conduct of a man in relation to his neighbors and friends, in the course of his business activities, and by way of the improvement of society and country. Hence, after enumerating many of them—for example, do not be a talebearer, do not be vengeful, do not stand by as your brother's blood is shed, do not curse the deaf, stand up for an aged individual, and so on—there is formulated the general principle that a man shall do that which is good and right in everything. Included under this rubric is compromise; where compassion is appropriate, going beyond the letter of the law, etc.[5]

The point is that it is left to human sensibilities and human conceptions to provide a basis for the formulation of the supplementary principles which will express that which is good and right. Even if such new rules of conduct represent an attempt by the sages to extrapolate from biblically recorded precepts and to infer from them others which would be applicable to noncovered instances, the human and, hence, secular element could not be eliminated. The halakhah includes both *din*, precepts of law, and *lifnim mishurat hadin*, a general principle which requires, for example, that a precept of law which in its strict application would favor a prosperous litigant be set aside in certain instances to assist the disadvantaged. And even while both are divine imperatives, the human element cannot be excluded. The judge must determine, on the basis of human considerations, when to apply either of these principles. The parameters of *lifnim mishurat hadin* are not explicitly formulated, and even where they are, they reflect, in some measure, the human sense of what is good and right. In other words, the secular is frequently intertwined with the sacred in the application of precepts that belong to the sacred.

It is clear from the halakhah that many fundamental moral principles can be perceived to possess a secular as well as a sacred basis. A clear distinction is made in rabbinic literature between *mishpat*, the rational precept, and *ḥok*, the nonrational commandment. "Thou shalt not kill" and "Thou shalt not steal" are imperatives which man could have formulated and applied in the context of social life without divine intervention. These are rational laws and are to be distinguished from such rules of action as "Do not work on the Sabbath day" or "No bread may be consumed during the festival of Passover," which are nonrational in character.

Obviously, nonrational precepts require a transcendental source to give them sanction. They could not have been deduced from the human condition. The rational precepts, on the other hand, may find their basis in either domain—the sacred or the secular. This was stressed, among others, by Rabbi Meir Simcha HaCohen, who declared that the moral laws are imprinted in the very nature of man, who could have discovered them without recourse to revelation.[6] It follows that one might be responsive to a given imperative (e.g., "Thou shalt not steal") either because of a commitment that flows from the domain of the sacred or because of one that flows from the secular. It is a halakhic requirement that when a pattern of conduct is sanctioned by both domains, the Jew select as his source of motivation the transcendental command. Notwithstanding, there is, as well, a human, and hence a secular, basis for ethical precepts, and this is recognized in halakhah.

II

There are two distinct sets of human virtues: one is associated with service and the other with creativity, i.e., one is deduced from the domain of the sacred and the other from the secular. The traits of character essential for service are, for example, dedication, love, selflessness, and so on. Qualities that are indispensable for creativity are industry, intellectual acumen, drive, etc. These virtues are very often lumped together under the rubric of moral character, but they need to be distinguished.

Samson R. Hirsch noted that the virtues that are praised in the classroom do not necessarily contribute to the development of moral character, i.e., they do not encourage conduct in relation to others that conforms to accepted moral precepts.[7] The student is taught to work, to compete, to cultivate effective study habits, to develop those intellectual abilities that will enable him to master a subject and achieve good grades. What have these traits, Hirsch asked, to do with the moral precepts which instruct an individual how to behave to his fellow man? In fact, Hirsch notes, some of the qualities advocated for the student in the classroom are incompatible with the cultivation of the kind of moral quality that makes for constructive human relations. The competitive spirit, for example, while laudable in preparation for examinations, is very often inimical to an acceptable response to those who are afflicted and oppressed. Competition is an exercise that strengthens the tendency to strive for personal success rather than to give of oneself unselfishly in fulfillment of a religious objective.

In truth, there is a variety of groups of virtues, each deducible from a different ideal. The ideal of morality requires such character traits as compassion, honesty, charity, etc.; the ideal of creativity calls for determination, industry, the cultivation of talent, etc.; the goal of piety calls for dedication, sacrifice, etc. We will identify the virtues associated with creativity as secular and those deduced from the religious ideal as sacred. The moral virtues will be regarded as secular or as sacred depending on whether our commitment to them is based on secular or religious considerations.

It is clear that the secular virtues deduced from the ideal of creativity are not rejected in the religious perspective. On the contrary, they are indispensable to achievement in the religious domain. Students are encouraged to study in a yeshiva and are rewarded for outstanding personal success. To stump the Rebbe, i.e., to ask a *kashe* (a question which identifies a difficulty in a talmudic passage) which the Rebbe cannot answer, is regarded as a most admirable accomplishment. This virtue has nothing to do with those associated with the sacred, which stress personal sacrifice rather than personal achievement.

In addition, there is a clear appreciation in biblical and rabbinic literature of secular virtues in the pursuit of secular objectives. There is a striking passage in the Book of Proverbs which urges man to take an example from the ant, which is hard-working and industrious and consequently successful.[8] The rabbinic precept, "The combination of Torah with worldly occupation is beautiful,"[9] implies that one should develop the traits that will assure fulfillment in the pursuit of both. Obviously, human traits essential for human creativity are virtues found praiseworthy by Judaism. After all, in engaging in such creative pursuits in the natural domain, man is imitating his Creator, and is not this his obligation in virtue of the fact that he was created in His image?

IV

In truth, all will grant that the pursuit of creative goals and the practice of secular virtues are commendable when they are motivated by religious considerations. One may argue, for example, that the cultivation of intellectual acumen is essential for the satisfactory comprehension of Torah, the study of which is indispensable for a relationship with God. Or, if one adopts the point of view of Rabbi Joseph B. Soloveitchik, he may urge that when an individual engages in creative activity or cultivates the virtues essential for it and does so in fulfillment of the divine imperative of *vekhivshuha*, i.e., to exercise control over the natural universe, the secular activity in which he immerses himself has halakhic sanction, because by its means he manifests the image of God.

The question is: Is there any religious value, from the standpoint of halakhah, to creative activity and the practice of virtues that are implied by it when the motivation for such action is entirely unrelated to religious inclinations? Suppose a person engages in the practice of medicine or, as an engineer, constructs housing for the members of society but does this out of sheer human sensitivity or because of a sense of personal satisfaction that he derives from achievement, would halakhah attach any positive value to his activity?

The issue is discussed in explicit form by Maimonides. In speaking of those who have assumed the obligation to abide by the seven Noachide commandments, he suggests that these duties may be undertaken for two different types of reasons. One is religious, i.e., they are recognized as imperatives having divine sanction and are accepted as a matter of obedience to the Divine Will; the other is rational, i.e., they are acknowledged to be prescriptions of reason which every human being is obligated to obey. What status, from the halakhic standpoint, is assigned to one who accepts the Noachide commandments out of rational rather than religious considerations? There are two versions of what Maimonides says. One text reads as follows:

> All who accept the seven commandments and are careful to observe them are to be counted among the pious gentiles, and they have a share in the world to come. This, however, is the case only if they accept them and observe them because God commanded them in the Torah and informed us through our teacher Moses that the children of Noah were long ago commanded to observe them. However, if one observes them because he is rationally persuaded, then he is not a *ger toshav* (resident convert) and is not among the pious of the gentiles *but only of their wise men.*[10]

I have italicized the last phrase because it appears in another version in other editions. The alternative formulation is: "nor of their wise men." It seems obvious, on the first version, that an individual prompted to observe the Noachide precepts on rational grounds, though he is not to be regarded as a resident convert or a pious individual, should be accorded the respect due to one who is a wise man. Accordingly, the inclination to do the right things for reasons which are not at all religious is still admirable in the halakhic perspective. On the second version, which denies wisdom to such an individual, it might be argued that Maimonides does not view with respect one whose motivation for adhering to the prescribed precepts is merely rational and therefore secular.

There is, however, a second possible interpretation of the second version. One of the Noachide commandments is the belief in God. Once an individual adopts this belief on rational grounds, he should be prepared to accept the obligation to observe the Noachide precepts on a religious basis. Since the truth of God's existence has been demonstrated (in the days of Maimonides, it was generally accepted that this was the case), and the assumption is that it is the God of traditional religion whose presence was rationally exhibited, it is an equally rational gesture to undertake the fulfillment of moral precepts on religious grounds. The determination to adhere to these precepts on an exclusively rational basis reveals a person who is lacking in wisdom.

It is well known that in the era of Maimonides, it was the general view that reason provided an alternative path to belief in God, and that revelation was not the exclusive means of doing so. Reason, accordingly, should have been used by the wise man to the end of adopting a religious commitment. The failure to do so indicated a deficiency in wisdom. In modern times, the view that reason is adequate to the task of revealing the truths of religion is no longer held. If today an individual, on rational grounds, arrives at moral conclusions that are consistent with the views of religion, it is not unlikely that he would have been viewed by Maimonides as a wise man though he did not relate his commitments to religious considerations—and this even on the second version of the paragraph adumbrated.

And after all, why should this not be the case? The Talmud attributes value to doing the right things for the wrong reasons. This is the principle of *shelo lishma*, which in effect states that it is desirable that a person's actions always be prompted by religious commitments but that those whose deeds are prompted by alternative considerations are to be valued as well.[11] It would appear that this principle should also be applicable to those who are inspired to perform moral actions for rational, i.e., secular, considerations.

V

The essence of the secular attitude is creativity in the human world and by way of application of criteria and goals that derive from the human condition. It is a realm in which we necessarily need to be involved even if we are satisfactorily to fulfill religious obligations. It can be argued, however, and with a great deal of cogency, that the halakhah finds merit in the pursuit of the secular enterprise, i.e., creativity and the cultivation of character traits associated with it, even when such activity is motivated by incentives that are unrelated to religious considerations.

4

The Sacred

An appropriate human response to the sacred is primarily the maintenance of distance, the removal of oneself from that which is sacred.[1] This is an attitude that, as a matter of fact, people normally adopt toward the sacred; it is also the posture that, by way of obligation, the Torah requires of the individual who seeks a relationship to the sacred. Ontologically, God, who is the source of all that is sacred, is described as completely other; i.e., there is nothing in human experience and language in terms of which He can be described. All of our verbal apparatus relates to and derives from experience, and consequently we lack the capacity to characterize anything that differs radically from the elements of experience. This is the essence of ontological distance, which, in effect, implies psychological distance as well. The latter is sensed as a feeling of helplessness when confronting the task of making clear the essential nature of God. In short, that which is Ultimately Sacred cannot be approached, and therefore, and as a matter of fact, God is removed from man, who inevitably experiences a sense of distance both ontologically and psychologically. In addition, both biblical and rabbinic literature impose on the individual the obligation to remain removed from the sacred. This is an expression of the imperative to exhibit reverence in the presence of the sacred.

In truth, there are two dimensions to the sacred which parallel the two aspects of the Divine Being. There is the *deus absconditus*, God as He is in Himself, and the *deus revelatus*, God as He reveals Himself in the universe. The holiness of *deus absconditus* is beyond the human capacity to experience. We are limited to the task of relating to the *deus revelatus*, to God as He reveals Himself in nature, and to apprehending the sanctity that we discover in virtue of that revelation.

We shall be concerned with aspects of sanctity which characterize its revealed form and which are Jewish in essence.

I

It should be noted that, on the Jewish view, sanctity is a character of things in nature as well as of the Divine Being. This may be viewed as a consequence of the two types of sanctity described above—one attributable to God as He is in Himself, and the other to certain manifestations of the revealed God. The sanctity of things in nature derives from these revelations. God reveals Himself in both creation and prophecy, and both constitute relations between God and the universe. Creation relates God to nature, and prophecy relates God to man. Now, under certain conditions soon to be delineated, when a relationship between God and certain elements in nature exists, holiness becomes a character of those elements as well. For example, we speak of the sanctity of the Jewish people. This sanctity derives from the special relationship that this people has to God. In this instance, holiness is to be attributed to both terms of the relation, namely, the revealed God and the Jewish people. The point is that it is not God alone who is described as holy; the people, in virtue of its association with God, is holy as well.

The concept of the relationship needs to be elaborated. Clearly, everything in the universe is related to God as His creation, but not all things are holy. What is intended is that anything which is a source of obligations in virtue of its relationship with the Divine Being, when other things of an identical or similar nature are not, is for that very reason sacred. The people of Israel are biologically like all other human beings; what distinguishes them is that being a Jew is a source of obligations—613 of them—most of which other peoples, on the Jewish view, do not have. The Sabbath or festival day, as a temporal span, is no different from any other twenty-four-hour period; what sets it apart is the fact that obligations have been associated with it which other similar time periods do not have. The land of Israel and the city of Jerusalem are, from a geological and chemical standpoint, identical in character to other portions of the globe. What makes them unique is that the Jewish resident of these domains experiences obligations—for example, the laws of the Torah that are dependent on land—which are not associated with other areas of the world.

We can accordingly refine our definition of a sacred object. An object in the realm of nature is holy if it is involved in a relationship with God such that the result of that relationship is that the object—the Jewish people, the Sabbath or festival day, the land of Israel, Jerusalem—becomes a source of religious obligation.

This conclusion reveals immediately one aspect of the nature of the holy in the Jewish perspective. The attribution of sanctity to an object in nature does not require the presence of God but rather a relationship with God such that the object imposes obligations. It is useful to note once more that there are two varieties of sanctity that reflect the two aspects of Divinity. The holiness that is characteristic of the hidden God as He is in Himself is invariably a concomitant of His presence. God appeared on Mount Sinai and uttered the Ten Declarations. The mount was treated as a holy object, but this status was merely temporary. The presence of God invested the mountain, but only for a brief period, with sacred status. When God withdrew from the mountain, its secular status was restored. The other variety of sanctity depends on an obligation generating relationship with God and is not a function of His presence at all. It is this type of sanctity whose delineation is possible.

A deeper understanding of this aspect of the nature of the holy can be gained by contrasting the *heftzah shel mitzvah*, the object with which a mitzvah is performed, with the *heftzah shel kedushah*, the sacred object. The etrog and lulav are mitzvah objects, while the tefillin, containing as they do portions of the Torah, are sacred objects. An obvious distinction between the two is that the etrog and lulav are not a source of religious obligation but rather the means by which a religious obligation, imposed by the festival of Sukkot, may be fulfilled; while the tefillin are indeed sources of obligation—even while they are at the same time a means for the fulfillment of a mitzvah. We are obligated to wear tefillin, but even while they are not on the person and hence a mitzvah is not being performed, they are sacred and impose obligations with regard to the way they are to be treated. But there is another and more fundamental difference. A mitzvah object, in and by itself, has no special status; it is and remains a secular entity. It is desirable not to discard irreverently a mitzvah object after its use in the performance of the mitzvah, but the reason is not the special status attained by the object but *bizui mitzvah*, i.e., it is derogatory to the mitzvah itself if the object with which the mitzvah was performed is treated in a disparaging manner.[2] It is, for example, unacceptable to discard the etrog together with other waste products, but it is entirely appropriate to turn it into marmalade and to consume it, for the latter procedure does not constitute an act of disrespect to the mitzvah. A sacred object, on the other hand, in itself, has a special status. The object itself is sacred and at all times requires special treatment.

There is another way of putting this. The rabbis distinguish between *ḥovot gavra*, an obligation imposed on an individual, and *ḥovat ḥeftzah*, an obligation deriving from an object. The requirement to use an etrog and lulav is addressed to the individual Jew—it is an obligation of the person; the obligation to stand in the presence of the Torah derives from the status of the Torah—it is an obligation based in an object.

This will explain why other objects with which obligations are associated are not in themselves sacred. A Jew has obligations with respect to nonkosher animals—he must avoid consuming them—but they are not holy. Such animals merely provide occasions for the fulfillment of obligations; they do not impose them. The reason is that such objects are not endowed with any special status; the obligation does not derive from the object but is imposed on the individual Jew. It is a *ḥovat gavra*.

We can now further refine our conception of the holy when that term is used to characterize objects because of their relationship to the Divine Being. An object is sacred when it is a source of religious obligation in virtue of its own status, i.e., when it does not merely provide an occasion for the fulfillment of a mitzvah but rather imposes obligations. It accordingly makes available opportunities, by means of the fulfillment of these obligations, for the service of God.

II

The discussion in the preceding section reveals an interesting aspect of the relationship between the sacred and the secular. It can be summarized as follows: That variety of sanctity which results from relation to the Divine Being belongs to objects in nature. Hence, natural objects can themselves be sacred and, indeed, are the only things, in the universe with whose sanctity we are familiar. But the realm of nature is primarily the domain of the secular, i.e., it is the domain of individual creativity. It follows that the only kinds of objects with whose sanctity we are familiar are originally secular and, further, that such an object can be sanctified by bringing it into relation with God in such a way that, by virtue of its status, it becomes a source of religious obligations.

A few illustrations will be revealing. Ink, whose chemical constituents are well known, is used to write the Torah on parchment derived from the hides of animals. The ink and the parchment are now sacred, for they are a source of obligation, i.e., we are required to behave toward them in a manner that is not appropriate to other samples of ink on parchment. A Jew decides to increase the time period during which he will observe the Sabbath. He performs an act of sanctification, i.e., he recites a certain passage from the Psalms which expresses a song in honor of the Sabbath, and as far as he is concerned, the Sabbath has arrived. A chunk of time prior to sunset on Friday is now sacred for him, i.e., it is a source of all the essential Sabbath obligations with which the Sabbath day itself is invested. Thus, ink and scroll and a space of time, basically secular entities, have become sacred.

This principle, namely, that the realm of the sacred with which we are familiar is to be found in the realm of nature, is a more accurate way of stating the popular judgment that Judaism is this-worldly rather than other-worldly. This assessment of Judaism, while well known, is often misinterpreted. It is given a hedonistic connotation which is entirely alien to the spirit of halakhah and Jewish life. It is therefore necessary to stress that its essential meaning is that Judaism focuses on that aspect of the holy which derives from *relation* with God rather than on that which is *inherent* in God. Consequently, while those whose religious attention is directed to the nature of the Divine Being as He is in Himself adopt an otherworldly perspective, Judaism, because its preoccupation is primarily with relation to God, is more comfortable with one that is this-worldly.

The notion of this-worldliness, which in effect is another way of saying that the religious goal of the Jew is to transform the secular by introducing into it a sacred dimension, has several ramifications which deserve elaboration.

First, sacred objects in the domain of nature call for action rather than contemplation. The approach to the sacred, it is now clear, is twofold. It may involve an attempt to reach out to the Divine Being and to apprehend, in some way, the sanctity inherent in Him—an enterprise which we have argued is beyond human capacity. God, as well as the sanctity that is His, is inscrutable. Notwithstanding, this approach is adopted by mystics. On the other hand, the approach to the sacred may be guided by the recognition that the goal of the religious personality is to bring things in this world into relation with God, an enterprise which requires action rather than contemplation. The two types of sanctity are polar opposites. One demands that we turn heavenwards to the celestial, transcendental domain, and the other that we focus our attention on the lower, terrestrial realm. If one adopts the approach of the mystic, his goal must be exclusively to *contemplate*, to experience, to be in touch with the sacred—indeed there is nothing else that he can do; if he opts for the halakhic approach, his objective is to act in a manner that will create the sacred. In the Jewish perspective, the terrestrial world is the locus of religious activity. It is there that we create sanctity by bringing things into relation to God.

For a genuinely religious individual, it is not easy to adopt the halakhic as distinguished from the mystical approach. Religious yearning would normally prompt an attempt to reach intimacy with

Him in the highest degree. A religious person tries to maximize his religious experience. The preservation of distance in his relationship to the Divine Being is for him a lasting source of frustration. He rejoices in contact. Notwithstanding, the halakhah requires this-worldliness; it demands that the Jew immerse himself in the world of human experience to generate sanctity. The halakhah mandates that, whatever else a pious Jew may be driven to do in the name of religion, he involve himself in the secular world in which alone religious action is possible.

Rabbi Joseph B. Soloveitchik distinguished between the distinctive and unique halakhic man and the religious man in general. He explained that while the religious personality attempts to elevate man to God, the halakhic man strives to bring God down to earth.[3] Halakhic man does this, it should be added, by bringing the things of this world into relation with God, thereby creating sanctity within the universe of nature. The fundamental category which lies at the basis of sanctity, in the perception of the halakhic personality, is that of *relation*—relation with God. It is the only access to God available to man. God, as He is in Himself, is forever and entirely beyond the human capacity to approach.

III

The ethics of piety, for the Jew, has its own character precisely because of the unique conception of the sanctity of the Jewish people which is rooted in the covenantal assumption of obligations which defines its relationship with God. The main implication of this attitude toward the sacred is that the Jew, while he attaches importance to and therefore advocates a posture of self-denial, finds no value in self-negation.

The difference is not difficult to clarify. To negate one's selfhood is to deny any essential value to one's human personality; it is to regard oneself, especially in relation to God, as intrinsically without worth. This attitude at times emerges from man's perception to the effect that in virtue of his spiritual incorrigibility—for he is hopelessly entangled in sin—his very existence is of negative rather than positive significance. The approach of self-denial, on the other hand, allows the attachment of value to man, even in relation to the Divine Being; it merely requires the denial of human impulses and desires the satisfaction when these conflict with the will of God. Self-negation involves the nullification and obliteration of the self; self-denial allows its affirmation so long as the individual succeeds in transcending himself in the interest of serving God.

But further, the attitude of self-affirmation is exhibited, primarily, and in its highest form, precisely in the gesture of self-denial. In resisting the urgings of his impulses and preventing their satisfaction in the interests of responding to God's will, i.e., by seeking to appropriate into his very being that which he regards as of supreme value, even when it contradicts his emotional proclivities, he experiences his self as elevated and ennobled. This is self-affirmation par excellence.

Rabbi Joseph B. Soloveitchik describes the religious personality who is responsive to the Divine Will as finding redemption in the very process of submission and simultaneously experiencing a profound sense of self-worth. He writes, "Cathartic redemptiveness expresses itself in the feeling of axiological security. The individual experiences his existence as worthwhile, legitimate, and adequate, anchored in something stable and unchangeable."[4] In redemption, the Jew achieves self-fulfillment in the highest degree and, accordingly, experiences the feeling of self-affirmation in the most meaningful sense.

This is neither a surprising nor an extraordinary conclusion, given that the Jewish religion is rooted in the idea of the covenant. To enter into a covenantal relationship with another is to assume that the parties to the covenant perceive each other as possessing power and responsibility. To undertake covenantal obligations presupposes that the individual who does so has the capacity to do so. It would be folly to attempt a contractual arrangement with a minor who lacks the intelligence or the capacity to assume obligations. The fact that God required of the Jew a covenantal commitment at Sinai clearly implies a form of divine respect for the human personality. Rabbi Soloveitchik goes even further. He argues that the covenantal agreement between man and God presupposes a certain relation of equality, namely, equality of rights. He writes, "The very validity of the covenant rests upon the juridic Halachic principle of free negotiation, mutual assumption of duties, and full recognition of the equal rights of both parties concerned with the covenant."[5]

The gesture of covenantal commitment, therefore, was for the Jew a supreme act of self-affirmation. In submission, he was elevated; in accepting the will of God and doing so in a covenantal manner, i.e., by mutual agreement, he was exhibiting a posture of self-respect and asserting a claim to self-worth that constitutes self-affirmation in the highest degree.

In addition, the acceptance of the covenant itself enhanced his sense of self-esteem. Through it, he acquired a degree of sanctity which had not been his heretofore. *Kedushat yisrael*, the holiness possessed by the Jew in virtue of his membership in the Jewish community, now became his inalienable legacy. He became a member of "a community of priests and a holy nation."[6] Such an awareness is the direct antithesis of a sense of self-negation; it does, however, ultimately depend on the gesture of self-denial that occurs in the act of submission to the will of God.

Accordingly, even the realm of the sacred requires the posture of self-affirmation. There is, however, a difference between the self-affirmation called for in secular activity and that characteristic of the sacred. In both, the goal is to appropriate value; however, the values obtained in the two modes of self-affirmation are radically different. The value achieved by secular activity depends on creativity and success; that acquired by relation to the sacred is revealed in a perception of self-worth.

The human being can adopt two different perceptions of himself and his essential nature. He can see himself as belonging to the animal domain. It is not difficult to do so, given the popularity of the evolutionary theory which holds man to be descended from the animal. Alternatively, he can see himself as one who is privileged to stand in the presence of and in relation to the Divine Being. The former is the secular view. One who adopts it may experience himself as of value because of his achievements and successes; further, he may identify this value with a sense of fulfillment, and assuming that he is motivated by altruistic considerations, a feeling that he has contributed to the well-being of his fellow man. But if his self-affirmation derives from his relation to God, he will experience a sense of self-worth that is independent of achievement but is rather the result of an assessment of himself as a creature of extraordinary significance because of that relation. Needless to say, for the religious individual, his sense of self-worth, given its sacred basis, is infinitely greater and his self-affirmation more pronounced.

What is even more striking is that the sacred basis for self-affirmation, even while it introduces a greater sense of self-worth than that derived from achievement, is generally consistent with the requirement of humility. If the ideal of humility requires that an individual refrain from regarding himself as of greater importance than his fellow, one whose sense of self-worth is based primarily and essentially on a perception of a relation with God will, in general, not perceive himself as better, at least for the reason that those with whom he compares himself are also, in his perspective, related in an identical way to the Divine Being. On the other hand, if his sense of self-importance is deduced from a feeling of achievement, he may easily be led to the conclusion that his worth, because of what is probably a biased assessment of his own accomplishments, transcends that of others—and this is the essence of arrogance.

Clearly, self-esteem is not uniformly to be rejected. In certain ways, it is not merely permissible but even desirable. The Talmud teaches, "Each man should say, `The world was created for me.'"[7] In the Ne'ilah prayer of Yom Kippur, we declare, "From the first Thou didst single out mortal man and consider him worthy to stand in Thy Presence." Rashi explains that as a result of such self-esteem, an individual will be prompted to avoid transgressions.[8] In other words, if a man perceives himself as an animal, he will behave like one; if he sees himself as a being for whom God created the world, his behavior will accord with his exalted view of himself.

It is interesting to note that in the religious posture, an individual finds a single basis, the covenantal relation with God, for the experience of both humility and greatness. On the one hand, in comparison with the Divine Being, he finds himself driven to say, as did the patriarch Abraham, "I am but dust and ashes."[9] On the other, he discovers greatness in himself in virtue of the fact that he stands in a covenantal relation to God. This attitude is expressed in classical terms by the psalmist who wrote,

When I consider Your heavens, the work of Your fingers,
The moon and the stars, which You have ordained;
What is man, that You are mindful of him?
And the son of man, that You visit him?
And You have made him a little less than the angels,
And You have crowned him with honor and glory.[10]

This passage expresses the sense that man is, on the one hand, totally insignificant ("What is man," etc.), and, on the other, exalted ("You crowned him with honor and glory").

The ethics of piety therefore calls for humility but also self-affirmation. What is required is a sense of self-esteem, the result of self-valuation, that is acquired through self-transcendence, i.e., submission to God's will, and the recognition that what is ultimately of importance is relation with God.

IV

It is now clear that, in the Jewish perspective, self-affirmation is a virtue rather than a vice. Judaism understands the value of self-denial but not of self-negation. Self-denial is entirely consistent with self-affirmation; indeed self-denial provides a crucial basis for it.

It is, however, essential, from the Jewish standpoint, also to differentiate between self-affirmation which is sanctioned in the religious posture and that variety of self-assertion which manifests itself in arrogance, which in the religious experience, is utterly rejected.[11] The self-affirmation whose central feature is the view that legitimate self-esteem is rooted in a relation with God which is the heritage of all in the community, provides no basis for the judgment on the part of any individual, no matter what the circumstances, that he is in any sense superior to his fellow man. Self-assertion, on the other hand, is a manifestation of the drive to control, to gain supremacy, to perceive human beings as essentially of functional or instrumental significance. This is the soil out of which arrogance, a trait repugnant to the religious mind, blossoms.

It is important to note, however, that arrogant self-assertion does not appear merely in the secular domain. In the latter it is exhibited in pronounced and often dramatic form—and with good reason. The secular realm is a sphere of achievement which is invariably measured by standards according to which people are normally judged to be unequal. One whose attainments are obviously more spectacular than those of others may easily jump to the conclusion that he is superior, not only in ability but also in intrinsic worth—with all the corollary attitudes that spring readily from such a posture, including the desire to exercise dominion over others. Obviously this is antithetical to the requirement of humility. Moral rules have to be introduced to counterbalance the inclination to treat others merely as instruments by which to realize one's goals.

The point that needs to be stressed is that self-assertion is possible in the realm of the sacred as well. An individual may arrive at the conclusion that his worth derives, not from his relation to the Divine Being, a character that is shared by all in the covenantal community, but from his greater achievement in the religious domain. Then we confront the entirely unpalatable phenomenon of arrogance rooted in what to the untutored eye seem to be religious considerations. In truth, while self-affirmation is crucial to the religious character, self-assertion is not; indeed it is repugnant to the genuinely religious mind.

But further, the confusion of self-affirmation with self-assertion is the essence of religious extremism and fanaticism. Religious arrogance consists in the importation of a quality that provides the basis for self-assertion in the secular domain, namely, success, into the realm of the sacred, where it does not belong; and further, to allow this feeling to express itself in pride. If, in addition, the success is of the communal variety (e.g., if a segment of the Jewish community has accumulated spectacular achievements in gaining adherents), self-assertion can be translated into triumphalism. Arrogant self-assertion and triumphalism are incompatible with the religious attitude.

V

In Jewish thought, sanctity derives from relation to God. This relation is entered into by the Jew by means of the covenant. As a consequence, the Jew, in virtue of his status in the covenantal relation, experiences an extraordinary sense of self-worth. The result is an act of self-affirmation, which in itself is laudable and desirable, so long as it is not translated into self-assertion. A true sense of the sacred leads to humility in man's relation to both man and God.

5

The Knowledge of God

What is the place of knowledge in the religious experience? Knowledge is of two varieties—the religious and the secular. The question needs to be asked with respect to both. There are those who would question the value of even religious knowledge for the life of religion. On the other hand, advocates of the ideals of *Torah umadda* and *Torah im derekh eretz* would maintain that even knowledge of a cultural variety is essential to religious living.

This question is particularly urgent in the context of the Jewish religion. The reason is its covenantal character; that is to say, it regards deeds rather than beliefs as at the core of the religious experience. The Jewish people entered into a covenantal relationship with God in which they agreed to abide by the expressions of His will in the form of mitzvot. Hence it could be argued that it is not a knowledge of the nature of God that is the object of the Jew's religious preoccupation, but the cultivation of an inclination to respond to His will. A study of God's existence or attributes may accordingly seem genuinely irrelevant to the pious Jew. It is for this reason that the question of the place of knowledge in the Jewish religion has significance above and beyond what it may have for other religions, in which the category of belief (a component of knowledge) is of greater importance than that of deed.

The focus of this chapter will be on religious knowledge, which essentially and ultimately consists of the knowledge of God.

I

There is a certain ambiguity in the religious conception of knowledge that needs to be noted at the start. In philosophic discourse, it is recognized that there are two varieties of knowing—demonstrable and verifiable knowledge, on the one hand, and a knowledge by acquaintance, on the other.[1] The first variety is normally expressed in the form of a proposition that asserts that something is the case. Its truth must be exhibited through deduction or, if one is concerned with material of observation and adopts an empirical standpoint, a process of experimentation. Such are all the propositions of mathematics and science. Knowledge by acquaintance consists in merely being familiar with some thing or some person. If I say that I know Mr. X, I need not be able to say anything about him. My claim need not, though it may, amount to anything more than that I have met him, that I spoke to him, that assuredly I would be able to recognize him if I were to see him again. I then have knowledge, but the knowledge which I have is not subject to a verification process because I affirm no proposition about him and, what is more, I might not even be able to do so.

In truth and by way of further clarification, it should be noted that the claim that I know Mr. X exemplifies both these varieties of knowledge. First, there is the assertion itself, namely, "I know Mr. X." This is indeed a proposition which affirms that something is the case, namely, that I know Mr. X. It is, therefore, subject to verification. Secondly, there is the object which I claim to know, namely, Mr. X. The object is not a proposition and is accordingly not available to verification. In saying that I know him, i.e., that I am acquainted with him, I do not make any assertion about him; I might not even be able to describe him if I were pressed to do so; I may have met him only casually and as yet be unable to form any specific views about him; and still I feel justified in saying that I am acquainted with him, i.e., that I know him.

The concept of religious knowledge has, in the course of Jewish intellectual history, been assigned both these meanings. In the medieval period, great theologians—Jewish and non-Jewish—defined "knowledge" for religious purposes in a manner identical to that given to it in the scientific domain. It was generally believed that it was possible to demonstrate (a process that confers even more certainty than verification) the existence of God. The celebrated ontological, cosmological, and teleological arguments were produced to establish irrefutably the existence of a Divine Being. Currently, such arguments are judged insufficiently cogent, and, it is claimed, other grounds must be found to justify the central thesis of monotheism.

We are accordingly led to consider the possibility of introducing the second interpretation of the concept of knowledge into the realm of religion. The knowledge of God is then to be construed as a knowledge by acquaintance, i.e., a knowledge that arises out of direct experience. It comes about via an encounter of an event or state of affairs which generates wonder in which I feel His presence without being able to formulate any propositions descriptive of Him or to say anything at all about Him. If I contemplate the totality of the universe and wonder about its very existence and the way it came into being, I may have an experience of God. If I consider the complexity of a human organism and marvel at the way each component combines with all the others in a remarkable organic unity, I may have a sense of a Supreme Being. When I think of the way a quantitative characteristic is transformed into one that is qualitative, as, for example, an electromagnetic wave of a certain frequency becomes a color of a specific kind, I have a feeling that this is a mystery which becomes intelligible only on the assumption of a Divine Being. Such experiences should not be construed as arguments demonstrating the existence of God, but merely as occasions which instill the awareness of such a Being.

Rabbi Joseph B. Soloveitchik directed attention to this means of arriving at a conviction that there is a Supreme Being through his distinction between the *ish hada'at* and the *ish hadat,* the scientific personality and the religious personality. When the scientist confronts mystery in the processes that he observes in the universe, he finds complete rest when he arrives at a universal law which enables him to explain and predict the course of human events. The religious person finds in that law itself a puzzle, a source of wonder—how was this law introduced into the grand design? and why this law rather than some other?—a state of affairs that presses upon him the sense that there is a Source of the cosmos.[2]

Even while this conviction is forced upon him, however, he is not able to describe that which he has discovered. He now believes that the Supreme Being is somehow responsible for the existence and character of the universe, for the beautiful, rational, and life-preserving arrangement of the human organism, for the transformation of sensuously vacuous mathematical traits into the rich colors, sounds, and textures of human experience, but he is not able to describe what He is or the process by which He has brought all this about.

The inability to cut through the experiential world in order to know, in the sense of being able to describe Him, the One who is ultimate in the universe was not unknown in the historical past. Even the rationalists of the Middle Ages—Saadiah and Maimonides, for example—argued that it was impossible to know the essential nature of God. According to Maimonides, one can successfully say what God is not,[3] or may draw some conclusions about Him from observation of the world He has created,[4] but no true statement can be made about the intrinsic nature of the One Who is categorically other and Who belongs to a realm which transcends the human being's capacity to describe. The mystics emphasized this point by insisting that the Divine Being is the *deus absconditus*, the hidden God.

We must go beyond this. Not only is God, as He is in Himself, beyond the possibility of description; one cannot even give a satisfactory account of the manner in which He relates to the universe. God created the universe, revealed Himself to the prophets, and will ultimately redeem Israel and mankind. Creation, revelation, and redemption are relations between God and the universe. No one has, indeed no one can, describe these relations, i.e., no one can give a coherent and intelligible account of the manner in which creation, revelation, and redemption occur. Creation, for example, refers to a process of producing something out of nothing, *creatio ex nihilo*. We know how, given the necessary materials, a house can be built, and we have the language to describe it. We have no idea whatsoever as to how to produce something from nothing; we do not even have a vocabulary that could serve to depict it. In short, We have no knowledge of God as He is in Himself, and we have no understanding of the way He relates to the universe; yet we know Him in the sense that we are acquainted with Him, He is familiar to us, we sense His presence.

II

On what is this confidence based? Perhaps we have deceived ourselves! There are certain features of human experience that give support to this affirmation. The first is the conviction that there exists a realm of mystery whose boundaries we cannot penetrate, but in which, we are nevertheless convinced, there exists a reality which has relevance to human life and the existence of the universe.

There is a sound empirical basis for the belief in the realm of mystery, though there are many who adopt it almost intuitively. It is generally granted that all our knowledge of things in the universe is ultimately based on the data we receive through our senses. Further, it is impossible, by the most powerful effort of the imagination, to generate an image of a datum which is radically different from any of the data of sense experience. It has been argued, for example, and quite cogently, that if a person is born blind, he is not able to form a conception of color, no matter how hard he may try.[5] The implications are that there are aspects of the universe which might be apprehended by mån in the event he were endowed with additional means of data appropriation, i.e., other senses, but which are now forever closed to him because of the limited number of conduits through which he acquires knowledge of things. It is a fair conclusion that there is much in the cosmos that a human being does not and cannot know. We might refer to the realm here described of the unknown and unknowable as possible sense data—possible in the sense that were the human being equipped with additional sense organs, he would experience a universe considerably richer than that with which he is currently familiar.

It should be added that a cosmos enriched by additional varieties of experience is also a cosmos enhanced by an enlarged edifice of science. If another variety of datum were available to sense similar to, yet essentially different from, those familiar to us, science would necessarily be expanded to take this new type of data into account.

For example, just as there are laws of color and sound as well as theories exhibiting the relations of these data to other phenomena, so would there be additional laws and perhaps other theories to incorporate into the structure of science the novel data. So we confront once more a realm of mystery, but in this instance, not the mystery of concealed data, but that of unrevealed science.

But both of these mysteries are such on the most superficial level. These are things that might have been available to human experience but are not for lack of sensuous capacity. It could be argued, and indeed some philosophers have done so, that there are deeper levels of mystery. In philosophic discourse, these are often referred to as the noumenal.[6] Even when the human mind apprehends certain data and succeeds in constructing, imaginatively and intellectually, certain hypotheses—its theories of science—the results arrived at are functions of the act of perception and the mental act of construction; that is to say, what we experience and what we know are ultimately dependent on the mind. When we ask: what is the nature of things independent of the mind, and how things exist in themselves, we are unable to answer. We are then talking about the realm of pure mystery. This is the domain of noumenon. Some have argued, and I believe with cogency, that the world of experience depends upon it; if noumena were not available, man could experience nothing, i.e., there would be nothing to experience. The religious thinker finds these suggestions appealing. He merely takes an additional step. Given the reality of these realms of mystery, it does not seem unreasonable to assume a still deeper realm, one to which God belongs, the ultimate cause upon Whom the entire cosmos—the experiential as well as the noumenal—depends.

III

There is another source for the human conviction that there is a Supreme Being—one that is psychological and emotional in character; to wit, man needs God. Particularly is this the case in times of trial and tribulation. In those intervals when the human being experiences himself as in control of his destiny, he may not be aware of an urge within himself to turn to One above and beyond him for solace and support. When, however, the tide turns and he finds himself *in extremis*, his sense of dependence on a higher being presses upon him. This is the kernel of wisdom contained in the expression, "There are no atheists in the foxholes."

This human emotional-psychological need manifests itself, in the most obvious and religiously meaningful form, in prayer. First and foremost, prayer is an expression of need. The individual may experience himself as afflicted—he may be facing a problem of health or economic well-being or a threat to loved one—and this leaves him with a sense of helplessness and a feeling that he has only One to whom to turn. This condition is articulated in the Psalms in a petition expressed in a state of desperation, "From the depths do I call upon You, O Lord."[7] Or it may not be a pressing problem at all but only a general urge to relate to One who is supreme in the universe, a relationship in which the individual discovers meaning and value, and which he expresses in prayer. We turn to the Psalms again for an illustration. "One thing have I requested of You, this do I seek, to dwell in the house of the Lord all the days of my life, to experience the pleasantness of the Lord and to visit in His temple."[8] In either case, whether it is a personal affliction or a desire for involvement with One who is ultimate in the universe, there is an emotional-psychological need which craves and finds fulfillment in prayer.

The sense of dependence and need leads man to a conviction that such a Being exists. From a purely rational standpoint, this is an unacceptable state of affairs. A rationalist seeks to adjust his feelings so that they correspond to a perceived reality. He will not allow feelings to serve as a basis for belief in a reality. He understands, for example, how one can express love for a person who is known to exist. He does not comprehend how an imagined being can be brought into existence by one's directing the sentiment of love toward it. This, however, merely enforces two obvious conclusions. First, any inference from a feeling to reality does not and cannot constitute a proof of the existence of that reality. Therefore, such an arrangement cannot serve as a *demonstration* of the existence of God. Second, a doctrine of rationalism which will not allow any consideration unavailable to proof as a basis for conduct or belief is inadequate for a religious commitment, i.e., a genuinely religious person cannot be a rationalist. He could argue, however, that while the claim that the absence of evidence to support the assertion that an object exists argues in favor of its nonexistence is valid without exception in the case of physical entities (which by definition should, to some extent, be observable), this is not the case with objects of a spiritual nature, which transcend the possibility of detection by empirical means.

Indeed, one could maintain that, in the realm of spirit, a feeling, an intuition, a direct though nonsensuous experience is the best means available to support the conviction that there is a Supreme Being. This suggestion has indeed often been made. One American thinker who argued in favor of the existence of God did so on an entirely emotional basis. He pointed out that what prevents many from adopting the fundamental axiom of religion is the *fear* that in doing so they may be mistaken. Those who accept the belief are encouraged by the hope that their longing for such a being may indeed reflect ultimate reality. He concludes by asking why anyone should be more impressed by the sentiment of fear than that of hope. He regarded hope as a more reliable and more appealing principle of human conduct than fear.[9] In any case, what is striking about this argument is that it is based on nonrational, emotional grounds which are perceived to be adequate as a basis for religious commitment.

IV

There is still another source for the conviction that there is a Supreme Being, and that is the feeling that the existence of such a being is indispensable to a meaningful life. For the man of religion, such meaningfulness is associated with a sense that he is part of a process that shapes human destiny. It is necessary to identify the distinguishing characteristics of the concept of destiny in order to exhibit the relationship between a concern with destiny and the religious response.

First, human destiny is associated with a goal that contains positive rather than negative content. Indeed, this is the basis for the distinction between a sense of morality and a sense of destiny. Morality, as crucial as it is for human well-being, is essentially negative in character. The precepts which command the avoidance of theft and murder cannot be construed as defining the goal of human life. There is nothing of a positive nature in refraining from actions that are ugly and that, if undertaken, merely impose a burden of guilt. But further, even the ostensibly positive gestures of contributing to the poor or defending an individual about to be assaulted or building a hospital to cure the ill, though undertaken in response to moral imperatives, remain negative in essence. Their thrust is essentially the elimination of poverty, pain, and disease. In a world without these afflictions, such actions would be totally irrelevant and therefore meaningless.

The difference between morality and destiny can be illustrated by examples from the Bible. The crime of fratricide perpetrated by Cain against his brother Abel, and the violence practiced by mankind during the era of the flood were moral transgressions. The Covenant Between the Parts drawn between Abraham and God to assure the patriarch that his descendants would inherit the land of Canaan, and the covenant at Sinai by which the Jewish people undertook to enter into an everlasting relationship with God by assuming the obligation to live according to the precepts of Torah are components of Jewish destiny. Engaging in the struggle to establish a homeland for the people of Israel in which life could be lived in a manner that embodies the values of Torah is not a response to a moral obligation, though the Torah contains moral content; it is rather an answer to the call of Jewish destiny.

Secondly, destiny is ego transcendent, that is to say, it is found, not in the isolated experience of an individual, but in a person's relation to something he perceives as above and beyond himself. In this sense, destiny is also to be distinguished from ethics. It should be noted that ethics is not identical to morality. The problem of ethics, classically understood, is how one should live in order to achieve happiness; while the moral question deals with man's obligation to his fellow man. Many responses to the ethical question have been proposed across the centuries, but, with few exceptions, their central thrust has been egoistic. The question is itself put in a way that suggests self-centeredness, namely, what ought a person do to achieve happiness, and for that reason tends to elicit a response that encourages egoism. Destiny, on the other hand, is dependent on self-transcendence. It has to do with the perception of something higher than oneself to which an individual is prepared to give of himself selflessly in order to realize values of overarching importance. Accordingly, solutions to the problem of ethics are generally found insufficient by the religiously oriented individual as an answer to the question of meaningful human existence, for they lack the selflessness that is an essential component of destiny.

Destiny is most frequently associated with a people or a nation. The individual belonging to either regards himself as an expendable part of a larger whole, all of whose members have as their vocation the attainment of a common goal which transcends the life of each. However, even when an individual speaks of a personal destiny, he is not referring to a state of affairs which will eventually bring him personal satisfaction and glory, but to an ideal to which he is prepared to subordinate himself and which he is ready to serve. Hence, even in the case of a personal destiny, the individual assumes a secondary position. Destiny, in all its forms, requires self-transcendence.

But there is still a third characteristic of destiny, namely, that the goals associated with it are of a metaphysical character. Their validity as goals is not based on human projection; they are not a reflection of human needs and desires, but are perceived as emerging out of hidden, invisible, and compelling factors which render their ultimate attainment inevitable. The metaphysical aspect of destiny may be understood as something that inheres in nature, as immanent, as an intrinsic force which necessitates a certain outcome—e.g., the claim, now largely discredited, that the proletariat will eventually rule the world—or as transcendent, as a goal ineluctably to be achieved because it was imposed by a Supreme Being.

The religious individual is not satisfied with the view that blind, unconscious forces could be responsible for the inevitable realization of gratifying and fulfilling human goals that come under the heading of destiny. Are there social or historical laws that can necessitate a process yielding social arrangements that would conform to all that destiny promises? Is it indeed the case that human beings, by undertaking certain goal-oriented courses of action, can in the normal course of events bring about utopia? There is little reason to assume that this is the case. Those philosophers, for example, who accepted the mechanistic hypothesis, namely, the belief that all events in nature are the result of mechanical laws, generally adopt an attitude that mankind's goals are not likely to be achieved.[10] Certainly, the religious individual is happier with the notion of a Supreme Being consciously intervening in the events of history to assure the desired outcome.

There is still another characteristic associated with the belief in human destiny: an optimistic point of view. One who adopts this viewpoint is convinced that the outcome is indeed inevitable and in all instances is prepared to act in accordance with this conviction. This belief, which leads to the very gratifying feeling that all is not a waste, that one's efforts and sacrifices are not irrelevant, enhances the sense of the meaningfulness of life. It is for this reason that the religious individual responds with so much enthusiasm to the message of Jeremiah, "Thus says the Lord: Restrain your voice from weeping and your eyes from tears; your work shall be rewarded."[11] This is a poignant expression of Judaism's optimism, a state of affairs that brings inspiration to the religious personality.

It should be noted that belief rather than an astute assessment of a situation lies at the basis of human optimism. Optimism is not rooted in facts. The general whose army is well trained, well equipped, and well fed, and whose superior forces confront an enemy which is inferior in every possible way, does not need to be an optimist to be confident of victory. Under such circumstances an incorrigible pessimist would probably share the sense of certainty of success. Optimism is based on faith, not on facts. The acid test of an optimistic person is his ability to maintain a positive view and sustain confidence under circumstances which do not lend support to such an attitude. The optimist, in defiance of the facts, continues to believe in the ultimate realization of his goals and ideals. It is obvious that, by this standard, the Jewish people is an optimistic people. It is also obvious that optimism is based on a sense of destiny, on the belief that the goals that we identify with destiny will ultimately and inevitably be achieved. The Jewish people is, therefore, also a people of destiny, a situation that, in the last analysis, derives from the fact that the character of this people has been fashioned historically by its relation with the Supreme Being.

When a study was conducted on the subject of civil Judaism, a large segment of the American Jewish community insisted on its identification with Judaism even while denying the fundamental axiom of religion, namely, the belief in God. The question was put to them: what does being Jewish mean to you? The answer was given in terms of a Jewish destiny in which they firmly believed but which they could not define.[12] It is reasonable to conclude that their sense of Jewish destiny, with all of its concomitant attitudes, is a legacy from generations past in which these were formed and blossomed in the soil of Israel's relation with the Supreme Being and the covenantal commitments mutually undertaken by God and the people of Israel.

The knowledge of God is not to be achieved by demonstration or verification. It arises out of an experience of which an individual is certain but which he cannot describe. Nevertheless, his conviction is supported by a variety of considerations. He knows that there exists a realm of mystery, that human beings are in need of a Supreme Being to Whom they can relate, and that such a Being is the justification for the Jewish sense of destiny which is a prerequisite to a meaningful life. He knows he cannot prove his belief in the existence of God, but he is prompted to believe in Him nevertheless.

6

Nature and the Religious Experience

Nature is central to both the cognitive and the aesthetic enterprise. Scientists explore it to acquire knowledge, and those with artistic inclinations seek to appreciate its beauty. The two, however, are not unrelated, and we shall be concerned with both in an exposition of the role of nature in the religious experience.

The issues that are urgent for us are not those that arise out of the tasks of acquiring knowledge and developing the techniques essential for the appreciation of art, for these belong to the realm of method. Judaism has precious little to say about the methodology of science, i.e., the rules that need to be followed if we are to arrive at verified laws and theories, or about the means essential for developing a sense of appreciation. We shall rather be concerned with the value, for the religious experience, of the possession of natural knowledge and the appreciation of beautiful objects.

I

We begin with the pursuit of natural knowledge, an enterprise which Judaism encourages and which receives enthusiastic endorsement in the philosophies of both *Torah umadda* and *Torah im derekh eretz*. It should be noted immediately that these two philosophies endorse approaches to this question that are radically different.

Torah umadda adopts a practical and pragmatic assessment of the value of knowledge. To begin with, such knowledge is prompted by the human desire to know; its possession satisfies a powerful human urge. An ancient thinker, for example, began one of his philosophic treatises with the declaration, "All men, by nature, want to know."[1] One practical aspect of knowledge, then, is the satisfaction that it makes available to one who accumulates it. But it is evident that the fulfillment of this human need does not, by itself, constitute a justification of the enterprise of knowledge. There are instances in which the human organism demands satisfaction and yet, with relative frequency, a moral imperative intervenes to caution the individual to refrain from gratifications which cannot be defended on moral grounds. If the knowledge of nature is to be prized, this cannot be due exclusively to the fact that it provides psychological satisfaction to one who accumulates it.

The very same ancient thinker, however, in another tract, maintained that knowledge is of value because it is by means of knowledge that the human being expresses and fulfills his humanity. Man, so the argument goes, is the only member of the animal species that possesses the capacity to think and know, and it is in virtue of this ability that he stands above the animal kingdom. The inclination to rise above the realm of the brute through intellectual activity has always been perceived by teachers of ethics as of great moral value because it makes possible a form of fulfillment that is uniquely and distinctively human. This experience concomitantly grants the human being the highest pleasure and is, by virtue of such fulfillment and satisfaction, of the highest practical significance.[2]

Natural knowledge has additional practical implications which, while perhaps more mundane, are not less significant. Knowledge leads to the control of one's environment, which, in turn, contributes to the improvement of the quality of life and a greater appreciation of the experience of living. Human life in the twentieth century, if not happier and more secure, is at least longer and more comfortable and, where human brutality does not intervene, even more pleasurable over a longer period of time. But even when we perceive the value of knowledge in terms of technological successes, ultimately its practical significance resides in the enhanced and additional satisfactions it makes available to mankind.

Rabbi Soloveitchik argued this point eloquently and cogently. He maintained that the fundamental mandate to Adam I is *vekhivshuha*, you shall exercise control over the universe. Such a capacity belongs to Adam I in virtue of his intellect. Rabbi Soloveitchik describes in impressive detail how man's reason enables him to fulfill his practical mission of exercising such control.

> The most characteristic representative of Adam the first is the mathematical scientist who whisks us away from the array of tangible things, from color and sound, from heat, touch, and smell, which are the only phenomena accessible to our senses, into a formal relational world of thought constructs, the product of his "arbitrary" postulating and spontaneous positing and deducing. . . . In his full resplendent glory as a creative agent of God, he constructs his own world and in mysterious fashion succeeds in controlling his environment through manipulating his own mathematical constructs and creations.[3]

Rabbi Soloveitchik adopts a point of view that is prevalent among contemporary philosophers of science. No claim is made that the theoretical physicist, in formulating his ideas about the universe, in fact describes it. The concepts of the scientist are not to be construed as discoveries of entities and relations that inhere in the universe. His formulae cannot be regarded as reflecting some structure that is to be found in the universe he describes. What he does has practical, not cognitive, significance. The result of his labors is not that he knows the universe but that he can exercise control over it. The pursuit of knowledge, even in the perspective of the theoretical physicist, is of merely practical significance.

Rabbi Soloveitchik argues that the same holds of other intellectual endeavors as well.

> Adam the first is not only a creative theoretician. He is also a creative esthete. He fashions ideas with his mind and beauty with his heart. He enjoys both his intellectual and his aesthetic creativity and takes pride in it. He also displays creativity in the world of the norm. . . . Adam the first is always an esthete, whether engaged in an intellectual or in an ethical performance. His conscience is energized, not by the idea of the good, but by that of the beautiful. His mind is questing not for the true, but for the pleasant and the functional, which are in the aesthetical, not the noetic-ethical sphere.[4]

In Rabbi Soloveitchik's view, then, Adam the first, who is preoccupied, among other things, with the accumulation of scientific knowledge, is motivated fundamentally by aesthetic considerations, i.e., by enterprises which will satisfy his quest for pleasure and satisfaction. His scientific labors, his creativity in the realm of ethical and social legislation, his resolve to produce objects of beauty and art are all prompted by the same practical goal, namely, the accumulation of satisfactions and the experience of pleasure.

It is important, however, to note the sense in which the divine mandate contained in the imperative *vekhivshuha* justifies the pursuit of knowledge on practical grounds. The usual interpretation, in the religious perspective, is that the pursuit of knowledge is pragmatically justified if it, in some way, serves the interests of Torah. It may, for example, be perceived as prerequisite to Torah. This is implicit in the dictum in the Ethics of the Fathers, "Without bread, there is no Torah."[5] Practical activity is indispensable as a means to the preservation of life and ultimately to the continued study of Torah and practice of its precepts.

In another interpretation, knowledge is practically justified if it enhances the life of Torah. On this view, it is not merely the baking of bread, the sewing of a garment, or the building of a house that is justifiable on practical grounds but also the creation of objects of beauty and art in order to introduce an aesthetic component into the performance of mitzvot. Human life could be preserved without a beautiful mezuzah, an attractive tallit or menorah, and an architecturally appealing synagogue, but the latter enhance and ennoble the life of Judaism and in this find their justification.[6]

Rabbi Soloveitchik, on the other hand, maintains that the justification of knowledge resides in the fact that it serves the needs of the individual and mankind. *Vekhivshuha* means that in the pursuit of personal welfare and social well-being, we are fulfilling a divine imperative. The practical justification of knowledge does not reside in its relation to Torah precepts, either by way of assuring the possibility of their study and their fulfillment or by way of enhancing the performance of mitzvot. It finds its vindication in being an activity in *accord* with the will of God.

It is not even essential, according to Rabbi Soloveitchik, that one who engages in cognitive activity should perceive it as a *response* to

God's will; it is sufficient that he see it as *in accord* with the divine will. The principle of *kavvanah*, which demands that, in the performance of a mitzvah, the individual should be consciously motivated by the desire to be obedient to the will of God, does not apply to behavior that flows from *vekhivshuha*, which requires of the human being that he exercise control over the universe. This may be inferred from a distinction drawn by Rabbi Soloveitchik in the following way: There are two communities to which Adam belongs— the community of interests and the community of commitment. Adam I belongs to the former. The members of this community seek at all times to satisfy their individual needs as human beings. Even when they enter into relationships, the thrust of each is the fulfillment of his personal wants. This view recognizes the fact that a primary reason for forming a community is self-interest. Indeed, this is the idea that stands at the basis of the concept of the social contract. People living in approximately the same geographic area seek to form a political association in such a way that the interests of each will be maximally protected. But the community created by Adam I is to be distinguished from the self-sacrificial covenantal community, i.e., the community of commitment, chosen by Adam II. Rabbi Soloveitchik elaborates as follows:

> The main distinction between the natural community of Adam the first and the covenantal faith community of Adam the second becomes clear. The first is a community of interests, forged by the indomitable desire for success and triumph and consisting at all times of two grammatical *personae*, the "I" and the "thou" who collaborate in order to further their interests. . . . The second is a community of commitments born in distress and defeat and comprises three participants: "I, thou, and He."[7]

It is only in the community of commitment that God is a perennial partner. In the fulfillment of obligations even to a fellow, the awareness of God should be ever present. This flows from two considerations. First, in performing our duties with respect to our fellow man, we are in fact discharging our obligation to God. Second, it is by means of the fulfillment of these obligations that we establish the relationship with God that is the goal of the religiously committed individual. Hence, the essential participants in this community are the "I," the "thou," and the divine "He." But God is absent from the community of interests. The latter is based on a calculation of advantage in which only another human need be taken into account. The awareness that the authorization for participating in this community—indeed, the obligation to do so—inheres in the divine mandate of *vekhivshuha*, should be ever present. The religious individual should be conscious of the fact that the enterprise of pursuing one's interests has divine sanction. Nevertheless, he need not perceive his action as a response to God's will. He need not see himself at that moment as engaged in a relationship with God. What he is doing belongs to the domain of the secular rather than to that of the sacred, Hence, the essential members of this community are merely the "I" and the "thou."

It is necessary to elaborate on the difference between behaving *in accord with*, as distinguished from *in response to*, God's will. One such difference has already been noted. The former does not require that God be involved in the relationship of community even while man seeks in that relationship to conform to His will. When the action is in accord, the relationship is dyadic—it involves only a man and his fellow man. When, however, it is in response, the relationship is triadic, because God is also an essential participant in it.

We must go further, however, and remark that God is supreme in that relationship. When the action is one of response, then the individual subordinates his will to the will of God. In such circumstances, man transcends his own needs, desires, wishes, and inclinations, no matter how pressing they may be, in order to do God's bidding. When it is an action that is merely in accord, it is man's will that is paramount. Further, when he acts in accord, he is pursuing his own interests; when his conduct is in response, his own interests are a matter of indifference to him. In addition, when he acts in accord, his relationship to God is merely intellectual. He knows that God is present and that He has mandated the task of exercising control over the universe for the benefit of man, but existentially, man is engaged in pursuing his own interests. When his action is in response, he is totally, i.e., with body, heart, mind, and spirit, involved with God.

This means that a genuine religious experience is possible only when the action is in response, not when it is merely in accord. The uninterrupted awareness of God and His mandate which is characteristic of an action even when it is merely in accord does not suffice to give it the character of a religious experience; what is needed in addition to being aware is that the agent's will be suspended in relation to that of the Divine Being because of Whom the action is undertaken, and that he be totally focused upon and preoccupied with the task of engaging God in an encounter. In other words, the religious experience requires a certain variety of unity between man and God—a unity resulting from an identity of will and purpose— which is absent when man's activities are prompted by considerations of self-interest. Such an essentially religious posture is normally available in prayer and the performance of mitzvot, and it is therefore in these activities that a Jew finds religious fulfillment. When, however, he pursues his own interests, even if it is accompanied by the awareness of acting in accord with the will of God, the result is not a religious experience. The fulfillment of *vekhivshuha*, even when it is prompted by the awareness that it is a fulfillment of a divine mandate, is not at all in the same category as prayer and the performance of the 613 commandments.

II

The approach of Rabbi Samson R. Hirsch's *Torah im derekh eretz* philosophy to the knowledge of nature is considerably different. It is critical to note that for Hirsch, "*derekh eretz* and Torah are one."[8] Hence the natural realm, which is central to culture, i.e., *derekh eretz*, in both a scientific and aesthetic sense, should excite a religious experience similar to that which is inspired by the Torah. After all, both the Torah and the universe are expressions of God's will. His will created; His will legislated. Both call for a religious response. The nature of that response differs in the various kinds of religious activities—prayer, the performance of mitzvot, Torah study, the experience of nature and its laws. In prayer, one addresses God; in Torah study, one tries to understand His will; in the performance of mitzvot, one fulfills that will; in the experience of nature and its laws, one appreciates His creations. There are varieties of religious experience, and, for Hirsch, the appreciation of creation is one of them.

This view is not unanimously accepted. Maimonides, for example, did not identify the appreciation of nature as a religious experience, but as a means to the love of God. He wrote:

> Which is the way to love and fear Him? When a man contemplates His wonderful and great deeds and creations, and sees in them His boundless and infinite wisdom, immediately he loves, praises, and extols, and is filled with an insatiable urge to know the Great Name; as David said, "My soul thirsts for God, the living God."[9]

Nature, according to Maimonides, is not something that provides for the possibility of a religious experience of appreciation; it is rather a means, a conduit, which directs man to God and the love of God. This is not to say that, according to Maimonides, nature cannot be appreciated. To the contrary, Maimonides discovers in nature "boundless and infinite wisdom." It is rather that such appreciation does not constitute a religious experience. What gives it religious significance is that it directs man's attention to God and inspires love for Him. We may put this another way. It is generally acknowledged that the love of God and the love of Torah, which is an expression of God's will, are important religious objectives. Since the universe is also a manifestation of God's will, it would seem appropriate to suggest that the love of the universe, when perceived as God's creation, is equally important for the religious experience. But this attitude is not incorporated in the Maimonidean scheme. The love or, better still, the appreciation of the universe as an expression of God's will is not, for him, a religious value. Its significance resides exclusively in its being a means to the love of God.

It is interesting to note that Rabbi Soloveitchik adopts a view not far removed from that of Maimonides. Rabbi Soloveitchik speaks of the difference between the scientific and religious minds in their perceptions of science. For the scientist, the laws of nature are conclusions of his investigations. The questions that he raises are fully resolved when the scientific laws he discovers enable him to explain and predict the course of events. For the religious mind, these very laws are a source of wonder and mystery. Where did they come from? Who introduced them into the universe? The contemplation of the laws of science thus leads the individual to God.[10] This, and not the function of providing for the possibility of an appreciation of the created universe, is their essential significance for religion.

Rabbi Samson R. Hirsch adds that the appreciation of nature accompanied by the perception that nature is a manifestation of God's will brings another dimension to the religious experience. One might say that such an experience is in a sense similar to, though not identical with, the love of Torah. For both nature and Torah are created by God; they are products of His will. Hence, they require similar responses, each of which is at bottom a valid religious experience.

The better to grasp the significance of appreciation as a religious experience, it is necessary to contrast it with reverence. Reverence is the appropriate response to the holy as appreciation is to the beautiful. The sense of reverence is manifested in feelings of awe, and the beautiful in a sense of appreciation. Reverence is a stronger religious expression than appreciation, for it is a response to the sacred. Indeed, appreciation is a posture normally characteristic of the realm of the secular, and to the same extent that the sacred stands higher than the secular in the context of religion, reverence transcends in importance the sense of appreciation. Nevertheless, it is a crucial insight of Rabbi Samson R. Hirsch that appreciation, in conditions in which there is a recognition that God is the source of the object of appreciation, is also a religious response.

Hirsch's view may best be illustrated by means of an episode in which he defended a visit he made to the Swiss Alps. He is reported to have said joyfully, "Now I will be ready to reply when I am asked in heaven: Hast thou also seen My own Switzerland?"[11] The thrust of this anecdote is that the aesthetic experience, because it is at the same time a religious experience, is in a meaningful sense obligatory—which it would not be if it lacked a specifically religious character. Maimonides would not have regarded it as mandatory. It is quite sufficient to recognize the "boundless and infinite wisdom" revealed in the order of the universe which leads to a love for God. Neither does Rabbi Soloveitchik require this experience; he regards it as sufficient to contemplate the scientific structure of the universe in order by its means to be led to God. Only Rabbi Samson R. Hirsch insists that an aesthetic experience of surpassing beauty is obligatory for the man of religion because it is a religious experience.

It is now clear why appreciation has not historically been viewed as of religious significance. Those who sought to maximize their direct involvement with the Divine Being were prepared to surrender the beautiful in favor of the holy, just as they were ready to forgo the secular in favor of the sacred. It is, however, part of the philosophy of *Torah im derekh eretz* that appreciation, inferior though it may be in relation to reverence, still qualifies as a religious experience.

Appreciation in relation to the universe can be experienced on several levels. One can appreciate the beauty of nature, the laws of nature, which like the principles of mathematics possess a certain elegance and make possible an aesthetic experience, or objects of art produced by the human artisan out of the materials of nature. Each of these, if the divine source of all creation is recognized in it, makes available to the human being a religious experience.

III

We turn now to the experience of beauty, another aspect of nature. The role that this manifestation of nature plays in the religious experience is understood differently in the *Torah umadda* and *Torah im derekh eretz* philosophies. Their diverse interpretations flow from their respective views, discussed in the preceding section, on whether appreciation can be characterized as a religious experience.

For Rabbi Soloveitchik, beauty is a *subjective* experience. Its value derives from the satisfaction it makes available to the spectator when he views a beautiful landscape or a work of art. The relevant passage has already been cited. "Adam the first . . . enjoys . . . his aesthetic creativity. . . . His mind is questing, not for the true but for the pleasant." In the experience of pleasure, he discovers the value of the aesthetic experience. That enjoyment is its justification.

For Rabbi Samson R. Hirsch, beauty is an *objective* characteristic. It is an inherent trait of an object. Beauty is not found in a psychological reaction of an individual; it is intrinsic to the object. It is independent of considerations of pleasure. It is something that is recognized as a value that lies above and beyond the human organism. In the appreciation of beauty, man demonstrates that he is able to transcend himself. It is therefore a propaedeutic to the kind of commitment that is appropriate in relation to the realm of the spiritual.

This is the point that is made by Rabbi Hirsch in connection with his account of Shem, Ham, and Japheth. Ham represents the life of pleasure, the seeker of enjoyments and satisfactions. Shem symbolizes the realm of the spirit and the posture of commitment that it requires. Japheth is immersed in the world of beauty. However, to the extent that the appreciator of beauty reveals a capacity of devotion to something higher, to that extent does the aesthetic experience, suspended between the hedonistic posture and the act of commitment, constitute a preparation for the life of the spirit.[12] For Hirsch, the aesthetic experience is a prerequisite to and a preparation for the religious experience. Accordingly, it contains inherent value independent of any pleasure it may afford. He writes:

> But nations also appear which use their forces in the service of beauty. . . . They are conscious of some higher ideal up to which mankind is to work itself out of its crudeness. Through grace and beauty, they foster a taste for more spiritual activities, music, poetry, art. . . . But the education of raw unrefined humanity to the sense of beauty is not the highest. . . . Only that which can elevate the mind to a knowledge of, and the feelings to recognition of, what is true and good in itself, leads a man to the heights of what he is meant to be.[13]

The sense of beauty, for Hirsch, is therefore a recognition of things whose value surpasses even that of self-interest. This recognition is a pedagogic step in the direction of eventually recognizing the Divine

Being in things of beauty. When that state is achieved, the appreciation of beauty becomes a religious experience. In the words of Rabbi Hirsch:

> You behold His work, you admire His creations, you search out His laws, you enjoy His blessings. . . . Therefore when you behold and wonder, study and rejoice, bend your knee and worship Him, the Holy One.[14]

According to Rabbi Hirsch, therefore, beauty is objective, i.e., its appreciation involves a recognition of something that inheres in that which is beautiful. We may take this a step further and add that, for him, beauty is transcendental. The religious individual perceives in a work of art, a landscape, or a musical score something more than harmony and rhythm; it contains an aspect of the divine. To perceive in a thing of beauty nothing more than an arrangement of lines and colors is to diminish the experience by reducing it to purely aesthetic components. The appreciation of the beautiful is at once more profound and more inspiring if the transcendental element is included in the experience.

This explains the force and significance of the talmudic precept which requires that the dimension of beauty be introduced into the performance of mitzvot. As the rabbis put it, "Make a beautiful tallit, a beautiful sukkah," etc.[15] The performance of a mitzvah is clearly a religious experience; so is the appreciation of a beautiful object when it is perceived as an expression of God's will. When the two are combined, the religious experience is deepened and enhanced.

7

Man from the Perspective
of Value

The religious view is that man occupies an exalted position in relation to other species. One who adopts a materialistic point of view
and reduces the human being to the level of an animal is not as
inclined—though he sometimes is—to attach unique value to the
human being. Doing so, however, is central to a religious outlook. It
is the aim of this chapter to identify the elements of value in the
human personality as they are perceived in the standpoints of *Torah
umadda* and *Torah im derekh eretz*.

It should be noted at the start that according to both these philosophies there are two attitudes associated with man that possess
value. One is a sense of dignity, the other a feeling of self-worth. Dignity is a relational conception. It does not refer to a quality that is
intrinsic to an individual but to a relation between the individual
and the members of society in virtue of which he perceives himself
and is perceived by others as deserving of honor and respect. The
feeling of self-worth, on the other hand, is one that a person can
experience in isolation. Rabbi Soloveitchik, for example, puts it this
way: "Dignity is a social and behavioral category, expressing not an
intrinsic existential quality but a technique of living, a way of
impressing society."[1] When distinguishing between Adam I and
Adam II, he attributes dignity to Adam I alone. Adam II is described
as possessing a sense of inner worth, an inherent rather than an
external relational quality of an individual

We may begin with the view of *Torah umadda* as expounded by
Rabbi Soloveitchik. Dignity, as he explained it, is primarily a function of creativity and freedom. Both are stressed In the following
passage: "Only when man rises to the heights of freedom of action

and creativity of mind does he begin to implement the mandate of dignified responsibility."[2] Of course, freedom as a necessary condition for the possession of dignity is to be understood in the sense of self-determination. If the free individual, as freedom is conceived in the context of American democracy, is one who does whatever he wants to do, and what he wants to do is very often nothing other than to satisfy his momentary impulses, then his conduct in such circumstances cannot be characterized as dignified. There is no dignity in incoherence and in action that is replete with contradiction. Such conduct does not inspire respect. The dignified person, in contrast, is self-determined, i.e., he acts consistently and creatively on the basis of his own ideas and in a manner that accords with his commitments. This too is freedom—not the freedom of indetermination but of self-determination. The latter variety is consistent with the posture of dignity.

The man of dignity does not submit to coercion; he does not capitulate to external forces. A slave has no dignity, because his conduct is invariably compelled by one whom he must serve; neither does the man who is subject to forces of nature over which he can exercise no control. Rabbi Soloveitchik wrote, "For life in bondage to insensate elemental forces is . . . an undignified affair."[3] The patient who is seriously ill and hospitalized often complains of having been robbed of dignity. This is due, not so much to the fact that he must undergo a series of procedures that he may find embarrassing, but to his helplessness and the recognition that he has lost, at least for the moment, the power to exercise control over his life.

It is dignity derived from creativity that is a manifestation of *tzelem elohim*, the image of God in man. Rabbi Soloveitchik associated the first chapter of Genesis with Adam I and the second with Adam II. The declaration that God created man in His image appears in the first chapter and not at all in the second. The implication is that it is by means of dignity rooted in creativity, the posture of Adam I, rather than through the sense of self-worth, the goal of Adam II, that the human being reflects the image of God. That image consists of human capacities that enable man to imitate the Divine Being in the creative enterprise.

It may be argued that the creative activity initiated by man in imitation of God which confers dignity upon him must also have moral quality. The primary characteristics of divine action, as understood by the rabbis of the Talmud, are moral in character. If the notion of *tzelem elohim* means that man must strive to imitate God, then he must try to mirror divine activity not only in its creativity but in its morality. The rabbis understood the ideal of *imitatio dei* as including both creativity and morality, but they emphasized the latter most of all. Indeed, when they defined this ideal, they directed attention to ethical considerations rather than those of creativity. "Just as He is compassionate, so shall you be compassionate, just as He is gracious, so shall you be gracious," etc.[4]

It follows that dignity, in the Torah perspective, is not a trait that is based on man's creative abilities alone. It is also manifested when the creative gesture is a responsible one. Satan is also creative. He can use the most advanced technologies to build gas chambers and crematoria, and exhibit his power to vanquish and control by putting to death millions of innocent people. The image of Satan is that of the devil. His diabolical cast presents the contemptible—anything but dignity. Creativity is genuinely dignified when it is, at the same time, responsible. Rabbi Soloveitchik put it this way, "Dignity of man expressing itself in the awareness of being responsible and of being capable of discharging that responsibility cannot be realized as long as he has not gained mastery over his environment."[5] In other words, to be dignified, it is not quite sufficient to exercise control; it is also necessary to do so in a responsible way, i.e., in a manner that reflects the image of God.

It may be granted that a secularist can also perceive the human being as dignified when he is creative. He bases that character, however, not on man's possession of the image of God, but on the human being's distinctiveness in the animal kingdom. He maintains that man rises well above the realm of the quadrupeds in virtue of his power to reason and to understand. His uniqueness among earthly creatures and his obvious superiority to them are the essential elements that confer upon him the status of a dignified being. We may refer to one philosopher who adopted this point of view. He argued in favor of a position of ethical hedonism which identifies pleasure as the only good. When asked to explain the difference between man and beast, since animals are also prompted by the experience of pleasure, he answered that human beings possess dignity, which manifests itself in the fact that they choose pleasures that are rationally more sophisticated, such as those of music, literature, and the visual arts.[6]

But on this interpretation, too, dignity is associated with responsibility. For in the last analysis, the sense of dignity is based on the judgment of value. It is not the *fact* that the human being possesses intellectual capacity or that he bears the image of God that accounts for his sense of dignity. It is rather that he perceives himself and, more importantly, is perceived by others to be of *value* because of these characteristics. The man who utilizes his inventive powers to destroy his fellow man rather than to help and strengthen him reveals by that very act that he places no value on human distinctiveness and accordingly forfeits, in his own perception as well as in that of others, that status and stature which a sense of the uniqueness of man makes possible.

In sum, creativity in a responsible way resulting from the act of self-determination is the essence of human dignity. But responsibility can be rooted in either of two considerations. It can be based on the perception of the uniqueness of man as a rational being (an essentially secular viewpoint) or on the fact that in the rational creative gesture man reveals that he bears the image of God (in the religious perspective).

It follows further from the circumstance that the sense of dignity is dependent on an assessment that is valuational in character that the religious man, who sees himself and is perceived by others as created in God's image, experiences a greater and deeper sense of dignity than does the secularist, whose comparable feeling is deduced from the observation that he is different from and superior to the animal. The view that God has made man "a little less than the angels"[7] is more elevating and ennobling than the judgment that man is better than the beast.

The secular and religious views with regard to the basis of human dignity imply additional important distinctions. On the religious view, as has already been noted, the element of responsibility is more important than that of creativity; from the secular standpoint, the reverse is the case. There is a difference between creativity that is manifested in technological achievements and that which results in the development of institutions which serve society and mankind i.e. in achievements that exhibit responsibility and possess moral value. If dignity is based on intellectual distinctiveness, then scientific successes which are noteworthy by virtue of their genius or magnitude will inspire respect, notwithstanding that humanity is not well served by them. When the first human being descending from a spaceship stepped onto the moon, a President of the United States declared that this was the greatest event in the history of mankind, though arguably, mankind has yet to profit from this spectacular success. Nevertheless the astronaut surely projected a posture of dignity that was strikingly impressive. If dignity is perceived as based on creativity that is reflective of the Divine Image, i.e., it is measured by the extent to which it manifests a sense of responsibility, then personal achievement, magnificent though it may be, does not have the weight that creative service with its widespread moral ramifications has in inspiring the respect of mankind. The religious individual would appropriately respond to the President of the United States that the greatest event in human history is much more likely that which occurred at Sinai when the people of Israel heard the Ten Declarations. He would undoubtedly add that any institution created by man which would contribute meaningfully to the implementation of these precepts is far more significant and impressive than an astronaut walking on the moon. Dignity in the religious perspective is much more a function of responsibility than it is of dramatic, though sometimes vacuous, creativity.

There is another distinction to be noted. In the secular perspective, intellectual creativity need not necessarily lead to a perception of the creative person as dignified. One may adopt, for example, a pragmatic view of the human being. One would then argue, as philosophical pragmatists have done, that the intellect is not an instrument which enables man to acquire truths about the universe; it is merely a means supplied by nature to succeed in the struggle for survival. The chameleon can do so by the capacity to change the color of its skin and thus remain secure from assault; man can do so by utilizing intelligence for the purpose of finding means of self-protection. The implications are that mental power and the ability to change skin color are in the same category. The human status of man has accordingly been diminished. He may be a rational animal, but the rational element is eclipsed by the animal component.

The secular view of man also often adopts a doctrine of determinism. It maintains that the human being, like all else in the universe, is subject to the iron law of causality, from which there is no escape. Man is not free and hence is ultimately without dignity.

Such doctrines lead easily to philosophies which have the effect of dehumanizing man. If man is truly not significantly different from the animal, and if he is, in addition, as determined in action as are the elements of the inanimate realm, then how indeed does he differ from the beast? In short, dehumanization is compatible with the secular standpoint. Such a doctrine nourished the ideologies of fascism and communism, and these are repugnant to any claim which views man as created in God's image, in virtue of which man, capable of free intellectual and responsible creativity, is a dignified being.

II

The philosophy of *Torah im derekh eretz* gives an alternative account of the dignity of man. Rabbi Samson R. Hirsch associates the *tzelem elohim* with the prerogative assigned by the Divine Being to rule over the universe. "For this `Adam' is to enter the created world as appointed by God to be its ruler and its master."[8] One of the interpretations that Rabbi Hirsch gives to the root of the word *adam* is "be similar to," as in *heyei domeh lo*, "be similar to Him." Adam is a "being whose whole mission consists in his being a `likeness of God' but who is to effect this likeness through his own free willed independent energy, thereby the representative, the deputy, the alter ego of the Supreme Being."[9]

To be like God, therefore, is not merely, as the Talmud explicitly states, to practice the precept of *imitatio dei*, the imitation of God, in moral conduct; it is primarily to exercise sovereignty over the universe. Hirsch takes pains to underscore that this does not mean that an individual may challenge God's authority and do as he wishes. On the contrary, in relation to the sovereign, he must remain absolutely obedient, though—as the *melekh evyon*, the earthly king, as distinguished from the *melekh elyon*, the divine king—he should impose his authority over all creation. Sovereignty is, of course, an expression and manifestation of dignity.

It would appear, therefore, that the essence of *tzelem elohim* for Rabbi Hirsch is the exercise of sovereignty as a representative of the Divine Being. The element of creativity does not appear to be crucial for him. It is noteworthy that the term *vekhivshuha*, which for Rabbi Soloveitchik means the exercise of control via creative activity, is interpreted by Rabbi Hirsch as the mandate to accumulate material resources with which to strengthen families and to advance the needs of society, which are in effect the functions of sovereignty.[10]

It should be noted that the sovereign, much more so than the creative individual, can perceive himself to be essentially a surrogate of God. Creativity is a personal, nonrepresentative activity. It calls for the use of an individual's talents and faculties, which are not enhanced by the circumstance that he may have been designated an agent to accomplish a creative task. The sovereign, on the other hand, can easily interpret his task to be representative, and as a surrogate, he must ever be mindful of the One Whom he represents. This representative function confers upon him a status and stature which, for Hirsch, is the main feature of dignity. Obviously, if this is the essence of the *tzelem elohim*, the creative activity of the individual plays a relatively insignificant role.

Rabbi Hirsch does not distinguish the basis of the human posture of dignity (which he defines in terms of sovereignty and majesty) from that which grants the individual an inherent sense of self-worth. The *tzelem elohim*, man's function as the representative of God on earth, clearly instills inherent value in man. But that same state confers dignity and majesty upon him, for according to Hirsch, the phrase *na'aseh adam betzalmeinu,* "let us make man in our image," refers to the external appearance of man, which is a manifestation of the fact that man is the representative of the divine. "The bodily form of Man already proclaims him as the representative of God, as the divine on earth."[11] But since such a form is publicly visible, it also provides for the possibility of majesty and dignity, i.e., a relation with members of society that inspires their admiration and respect.

III

For Rabbi Soloveitchik, self-worth is rooted in entirely different considerations. It is an inherent value, based on the feeling of having been redeemed, that flows from submission to the will of God. A full characterization of this state requires a description of the nature of the submission as well as the meaning of this variety of redemption.

Rabbi Soloveitchik uses a striking term when describing the gesture of submission. He refers to it as "defeat." The use of this term is not intended merely to achieve dramatic effect; its purpose is rather to direct attention to a very crucial element in this human response.

Defeat demands of Adam II a total submission to the will of God. "Redemption is achieved when humble man makes a movement of recoil, and lets himself be confronted and defeated by a Higher and Truer Being."[12] Both Adam I and Adam II seek self-expression. "Both Adams want to be human. Both strive to be themselves, to be what God commanded them to be, namely, man. They certainly could not reach for some other objective since this urge . . . lies . . . at the root of all human striving."[13] Both appear to seek to express themselves, to find their own selves, but while one does it through victory in the realm of nature, the other accomplishes the identical purpose through defeat in relation to God. In a sense, Adam II achieves victory as well, that is, he secures his goal of redemption through a relation with God. But for him it is a victory born of defeat.

And it is by means of defeat that redemption is achieved. That experience confers upon the individual a sense of self-worth, a feeling that all is well with him because he has discovered his existence to be of inordinate value. It is such because he is a member of a community in which God is the primary participant. In these circumstances, "The individual intuits his existence as worthwhile, legitimate and adequate, anchored in something stable and unchangeable."[14] For the individual, as distinguished from the community, ultimate redemption is to be found in a relationship with One Who is eternal and of Supreme Value.

This is so for several reasons. In the first place, the value we assign to ourselves is often a function of the value we assign to those with whom we are involved. A relationship with the One Who is of Infinite Value brings to us the feeling that we, at least to some extent, share in that value. This was a driving force behind those who espoused a theology of mysticism. They sought to merge and achieve *unity* with the Divine Being, for this was the ultimate that could be attained in the pursuit of meaning and value in the life of a human being. Even while halakhic Judaism frowns on the attempt to achieve such unity because it is incompatible with the Jewish doctrine of the unity of God,[15] it insists on the importance of *relation* with God, a concept that was pushed to the extreme by Jewish mystics in their pursuit of ultimate meaning.

But in addition, it must be noted that there are varieties of redemption. Its social form consists in being liberated from conditions of oppression, as in the case of the people of Israel when it was finally emancipated from its slavery in Egypt. Redemption is economic in character when a person or people emerges from debilitating poverty into circumstances of comfort and prosperity. The redemption that is born of defeat is existential in form. It is a response to the human need to share in eternity. It liberates the individual from the annihilation of death, from the sense that life is utterly meaningless because, as Ecclesiastes put it, "The end of man and the end of the animal are the same; as one dies so does the other; both have the same breath; man has no superiority over the animal, for all is vanity."[16] The human being desperately needs to believe that life is worthwhile, that the effort he invests and the pain he suffers are in some sense rewarded, that somehow his life has permanent significance. He achieves this conviction through defeat, through a relation with the One Who is Infinite. God is the only being who can lift man from his existential loneliness and give him the sense that he has been redeemed in an ultimate and eternal way. In defeat, the human being discovers immortality.

IV

It is now also clear why, in the view of Rabbi Soloveitchik, the senses of dignity and of self-worth do not coincide, i.e., dignity is not a satisfactory means for the achievement of a sense of inherent value. It is not that dignity fails to contribute altogether to a self-assessment that discovers value in man. It certainly does, for the sense of dignity is itself of inestimable value. It does not, however, generate that sense of self-worth that is rooted in a relationship to the Infinite which constitutes redemption in the existential sense.

The point needs elaboration. Why should not the sense of dignity translate itself into a sense of inner worth? If my conduct inspires respect and admiration from others, why ought not this also be reflected in respect for myself and in a perception of my own value? There is no doubt that such a translation in fact occurs. But it is a respect that is bounded; it is an experience of the value of self that is uncertain. The man of dignity pursues scientific discoveries, technological achievements, and the creation of aesthetic forms. It is universally granted that scientific laws are at best merely probable; the claim to absolute truth cannot be made for them. Too many have fallen by the wayside in the march of scientific progress. The products of technology and even masterpieces of art have a transient character; they will not survive the process of deterioration that is endemic to the universe or a cataclysm which may sound the death knell of civilization as we know it. Man's extraordinary achievements are uncertain, his truths probable at best, and his creations assuredly finite. The value that a human being can perceive himself to possess in virtue of his creativity is contingent, conditional, and relatively small. We can sympathize with the assessment of the author of that magnificent passage in the liturgy of the High Holy Days,

> Man comes from dust and ends in dust; he wins his bread at the risk of his life. He is like the potsherd that breaks, the grass that withers, the flower that fades, the shadow that passes, the cloud that vanishes, the breeze that blows, the dust that floats, the dream that flies away.[17]

Permanent value can be found only in the infinite and the eternal.

Unfortunately, the sense of dignity, in the general experience of mankind, is prized more highly than is that of self-worth. This follows from the human preoccupation with fame and honor. It has been noted that dignity is a social concept; it can be experienced only in the context of society. It appears that man may very well be a social rather than a religious animal. His social predilections are stronger than his existential inclinations.

Both victory and defeat, both dignity and the sense of inner worth, require a posture of heroism—but heroism is of two varieties. There is the hero of the battlefield who is inspired to his extraordinary acts of courage, more often than not, by a thirst for honor and a desire to achieve the sense of dignity. But there is also the quiet hero who lives in suffering, sometimes even as an outcast, but who finds strength, courage, and peace in the knowledge that the relationship to God, whom he has embraced, bestows upon him inordinate value. He has achieved the ultimate goal of the religious personality: existential redemption.

8

Halakhah and Mathematics

The relationship of mathematics to halakhah is a fascinating question. According to Rabbi Joseph B. Soloveitchik, the halakhah appropriates into its structure a number of the features of mathematics. Here is a passage taken from his *Halakhic Man* in which this point is stressed.

> The "movement" from quality to quantity, from experience to equations, which takes place in the real, empirical world, also finds its expression in the ideal realm of halakhah. . . . Not for naught did the Gaon of Vilna tell the translator of Euclid's geometry into Hebrew that "To the degree that a man is lacking in the wisdom of mathematics he will lack one hundredfold in the wisdom of Torah." . . . The fundamental tendency of the halakhah is to translate the qualitative features of religious subjectivity . . . into firm and well established quantities "like nails well fastened" (Eccles. 12:11) that no storm can uproot from their place. The supernal will is reflected in the mirror of reality and the mirror of the ideal halakhah, through the medium of objective, quantitative measurements.[1]

Why is this the case? What are the essential characteristics of mathematics that make it particularly suitable for the purpose of characterizing the life of halakhah? Rabbi Soloveitchik's answer appears to be twofold. The mathematical approach introduces quantification and facilitates the achievement of objectivity. The incorporation of these elements into halakhah requires analysis.

I

To begin with, it should be noted that quantification provides the best possible basis for precision. Judaism is a covenantal rather than a faith religion, that is it requires, in addition to an affirmation of belief, a behavioral response in consonance with the obligations accepted by covenant at Sinai. Judaism is accordingly expressed primarily in halakhah, i.e., the law. The formulation of law demands precision in order to obviate situations in which uncertainty would remain as to the requisite course of action. Ambiguity and vagueness in the formulation of law invariably leads to litigation and endless disputes with regard to interpretation. If Rabbi Soloveitchik's intention were merely to emphasize the fact that religious Judaism has the kind of exactness normally found in law, it would have been preferable to describe the halakhah as legal in character. Rabbi Soloveitchik, however, prefers the mathematical model by which to underscore halakhah's penchant for precise formulation. Why is this the case?

In the first place, the precision of mathematics is greater than that of law. Precision in law is a function of definition, for law must define its crucial terms. What is meant by property, the right of privacy, equality before the law, etc.? However carefully the task of definition is carried out, areas that are hazy and nebulous remain. Precision in mathematics depends on quantification. Deviation from the mathematically required conclusion by even an exceedingly small amount constitutes an error.

Halakhah strives for mathematical precision. The idea of sunset, for example, is associated in halakhah with an abundance of obligations—the recitation of prayer, the arrival of the Sabbath or a festival day, the point in time at which a person spiritually contaminated is restored to a state of ritual purity, etc. The halakhah seeks to pinpoint the exact moment when one day ends and the following day begins, i.e., it assigns a precise mathematical measure to the concept of the beginning of a day. And even while a difference of opinion arises with regard to this question—does the day start at sunset, or when the light of the sun disappears?[2]—on either view, a precise answer in quantitative terms is proposed.

Furthermore, law is burdened by associations which mathematics is spared. The intent of law is to compel citizens to behave in a prescribed fashion with the understanding that failure to do so would result in punishment. Law operates with threats instilling fear among those to whom it is addressed. The greater the precision of law, the more demanding it is, and the more ominous it is. Not so with mathematics, where precision is an ideal, an object of endless fascination inspiring feelings of admiration and enthusiasm. This is the posture to be associated with halakhah. The attempt to define it with ever-increasing exactitude through quantification is an expression of the love of God and the concomitant desire to come as closely as possible to the fulfillment of God's will. It is true that the Bible exacts punishment for transgression; its central thrust is nevertheless directed to performance rather than the painful consequences that flow from violation. By way of emphasizing this point, biblical literature even interprets pain attendant upon transgression as an expression of God's love—"Those whom God loves He chastises."[3] The use of law as a model for the halakhic system does not sufficiently acknowledge the very crucial positive dimension of mitzvot in the life of the halakhic personality. Mathematics is clearly a model to be preferred.

It is for this very reason that some Jewish thinkers attempted to distinguish the concept of law, as it is generally understood, from mitzvah, the halakhic term that denotes the law. They pointed to the fact that mitzvah is an expression of the love of God for man, as distinguished from law, which instills fear.[4] To accept law as a model for halakhah is to allow an unfortunate distortion. This is not to say that law and mitzvah have nothing in common. Indeed they do in that both make demands and both prescribe painful consequences in the event of disobedience. There is this crucial difference, however. While adherence to the law is urged upon the members of society with threats intended to instill fear, mitzvot as well as the suffering attendant upon their violation are presented, essentially and primarily, as expressions of love between man and God. The mathematical model minimizes the component of fear in the halakhic perspective.

Further, to allow conduct to be directed by rules that are expressed in a quantifiably precise way is to adopt the path of moderation. Moderation requires a measured response because it is a manifestation of rationality, and the latter, when it serves as a guide to action, calls for deliberate and, wherever possible, quantifiably defined behavior. Maimonides made this clear in his exposition of the principle of moderation, in which he emphasizes the importance of applying measure to conduct. He writes: "Indeed, moderation is truly very important. A man should always direct all his efforts toward attaining it and measure all his actions until he achieves moderation."[5]

Actions can, after all, be performed and their corresponding virtues exhibited in varying degrees. We may take generosity as an example. Some are more philanthropic than others; some contribute all they possess, and some are frugal to the point of never performing a charitable gesture. The varying degrees of generosity can be symbolized by a line whose points represent its different quantities. The rational individual, i.e., the one who practices moderation, strives for that degree which is represented by the midpoint on the line. The quantification of even the moral virtues which do not easily lend themselves to it contributes to the achievement of the goal of moderation.

II

Quantification advances the process of achieving objectivity, to which, according to Rabbi Soloveitchik, the halakhah assigns a great deal of importance. The religious attitude is most often associated with subjectivity, i.e., with feeling, emotion, and sentiment. The locus of the religious experience is usually taken to be the heart. Rational considerations are excluded because they limit emotional expression and because they generally have a pragmatic orientation which interferes with the affective thrust characteristic of those who seek contact with the Supreme Being. Yet, while the subjective component is indispensable to the religious posture, the objective element is, in the halakhic standpoint, even more essential. Two questions need to be answered: What is the relation between quantification and objectivity? Why is objectivity so important to religious expression?

In response to the first question, it should be noted that quantification enhances the translation of the subjective into the objective. A feeling, an emotion, is amorphous; it has no determinate shape; it is not subject to mathematical measurement. Different people experiencing ostensibly the same feelings cannot compare them even to determine whether they are identical, let alone equal. Feelings can be quantified only if they are objectified. The process of objectification begins when the covenant, as an instrument defining the relation between man and God, is introduced. Emphasis on belief elevates the importance of subjective thoughts, feelings, and attitudes. The covenant, on the other hand, focuses on obligations, fulfilled in the public domain, as the essential means of religious expression. This was the first step in the translation of the subjective into the objective—moving from subjective feeling to obligations expressed publicly in conduct. The second equally important step involved the mathematical characterization of these obligations. When beliefs and commitments are translated into covenantally prescribed actions that are publicly visible, and when they are defined quantitatively, it becomes possible to identify and to measure the religious gesture. Quantification moves the halakhic response further along the way to objectivity.

The remarkable nature of this translation of the subjective into the mathematically objective should not be underestimated. It will be appreciated if it is observed that there are two processes of quantification. One applies to objects that are extended, i.e., those to which the law of addition is applicable. If there are two groups of five apples each, their sum is ten apples. If the length of two objects is ten feet each, the total if they are placed in juxtaposition is twenty feet. The other process applies to intensive experiences to which the principle of addition does not apply. If the temperature of two objects is twenty degrees centigrade, the temperature of the two combined is not forty degrees centigrade. The latter provides an instance of an intensive quality which, though it is not immediately obvious, is available for measurement. Science took a major step forward when it discovered that intensive experiences are subject to quantification. It could then assign numbers to such things as heat by means of the concept of temperature, colors, and sounds by means of the concept of the frequency of transverse and longitudinal waves, etc. The measurement of intensive qualities enhanced the development of mathematical physics. The achievement was spectacular.

Beliefs and emotions are also intensive qualities. It is one of the significant features of Judaism that, at its beginning, it translated subjective traits of belief and religious feeling into measurable objective quantities, a circumstance that gives it its distinctive halakhic character. It did this by introducing the idea of the covenant, by turning the inner religious experience into an objective, public obligation to respond to the will of God and by interpreting these obligations quantitatively.

Now to the second question. Why is objectivity, achieved by quantification, so important? First, there is the psychological impact. How does one intensify religious sentiment and commitment? One could argue that the most effective approach is to make available a variety of experiences by which religious sentiment will gain in depth and meaning. One could, for example, try to turn every religious service into a consciousness-raising and emotionally exciting event. This appears to be the way of religious revivalists. The other approach is to encourage study in order to enhance understanding and to prescribe patterns of conduct which will shape character and mold personality. Many rabbinic interpreters of the Talmud argued that the reason that the halakhah adopted the way of mitzvot as the means of religious expression is that action is the best means available for instilling correlative feelings and beliefs.[6] It is a convincing thesis that the goal of implanting religious character in the human being is more readily accomplished by conduct than by making available appropriate experiences.

Rabbi Soloveitchik argued accordingly that if subjectivity is not translated into objectivity, the religious enterprise fails.

> A subjective religiosity cannot endure. And all those tendencies to transform the religious act into pure subjectivity . . . will in the end prove null and void. . . . A subjective religiosity comprised of spiritual

moods of emotions and affections, of outlooks and desires, will never be blessed with success.[7]

Somehow, subjective experience in itself is not quite adequate to the task. There was a time when the emphasis in the American Jewish community was on education. It was argued that if a child received a Jewish education, his Jewish identity would be assured. This constitutes what I have identified elsewhere as the intellectualistic fallacy.[8] When the Jewish community was awakened to the realization that education in its intellectual form is not a panacea, a new experiential approach was attempted. Expose an individual to a variety of religiously inspiring experiences to intensify his sense of appreciation, it was argued, and his commitment to Judaism would be assured. The results of this experiment do not justify optimism. The halakhah emphasizes the method of action informed by study as by far the best way to a life of religious significance.

Of even greater importance are the sociological ramifications of objectification. The personal individual dimension is, of course, perennially present. When one prays on the Day of Atonement, for example, he has a sense that he, as an individual, is presenting himself before the Supreme Being to petition Him for forgiveness and a good life in the year to follow. Notwithstanding, even on that occasion, the communal element emerges. In the confession, which is the crucial component of the Yom Kippur liturgy, the emphasis is on the community. The worshipper recites, "We have sinned, we have transgressed," etc. The Sinaitic covenant was drawn, not between God and individuals standing at the foot of Sinai but with the entire people. It is noteworthy that while the people was addressed in the singular, i.e., with the term "thou," as, for example, in "Thou shalt not steal," which is a way of addressing an individual, the people responded in the plural, "We shall obey; we shall listen," i.e., each person accepted the duties prescribed in behalf of all. The Sinaitic covenant was an acceptance of obligations in which each person assumed responsibility for the community..

The Jewish people is a community in a unique sense. A community is normally taken to be a group of people living in a single geographic area whose institutions define the norms of behavior for its members. The Jewish people, distributed as it is around the globe, is not confined to any area, yet the feeling of solidarity characteristic of a community prevails. One of the reasons for this is the substantially identical norms which provide the guidelines for conduct wherever Jews are found. The Jewish people is both a family and a community. The sense of family is based on the recognition of the importance of biological criteria for membership in the community. The sense of community derives from the awareness that Jewish guidelines for conduct are similar throughout the world. Were it not for the objective dimension of Judaism, the goal of community could not have been accomplished. The element of mathematical precision enhances the sense of community even more because it helps to highlight and dramatize identities and similarities.

The implications of this discussion for the halakhic view on the issue of pluralism are important. The adoption of pluralism as a way of life in the Jewish community is usually taken to mean the endorsement of all denominations of Judaism as halakhically legitimate. It must be stated, therefore, that the halakhah does not grant such legitimacy. To the contrary, given that Judaism is a religion in which objective obligations are more important than subjective feelings, and given that Judaism is essentially of a communal character, it follows that the greater the similarity, the more perfect the identity, in Jewish conduct everywhere, the stronger the sense of community among Jews. It is for this reason that the rebellious sage was condemned in the Bible. His sin in introducing a form of conduct that deviated from that prescribed by the Great Sanhedrin, the supreme religious body, whose obligation it was, when necessary, to define Jewish life for the total community, was regarded as particularly reprehensible.[9] As Nachmanides puts it in his commentary on the Bible, "We should not make the Torah many Torahs."[10]

The halakhah clearly allows a pluralism of thought so long as different viewpoints conform to certain guidelines. A variety of interpretations of biblical and rabbinic texts was always encouraged because of the obvious contribution that discussion makes to clarity and truth. The rebellious sage was permitted to disagree with the

Great Sanhedrin even after it stated its views.[11] He was, however, not permitted to render a decision based on his diverging opinions that would result in action incompatible with the decision of the great judicial body. Such conduct is not consistent with the needs of community.

It should be added, as a factual matter, that the rise of pluralism was due to historical circumstances. With the destruction of the Temple and the disappearance of the Sanhedrin, the power to restrain halakhically insurgent behavior was lost. Given the present state of affairs, it is eminently desirable for all denominations to coalesce into some form of unity to respond to the many challenges that threaten Jewish life. From a halakhic standpoint, however, denominations can receive only *de facto*, not *de jure*, recognition. It should be noted that the existing pluralism is the result of accidents of history; it is not an ideal of Jewish life.

III

Even while the halakhic accent is on the objective, the subjective component in religious expression is not to be ignored. The awareness of a personal relation with the Supreme Being is of the utmost importance. This is stressed in a variety of ways. When, for example, a Jew stands in prayer, he need not fully understand what he is saying and he need not focus on those in whose behalf he is offering petitions, but he must at every moment be conscious of the fact that he is standing in the presence of God. If he fails in this awareness, he cannot be said to be engaging in prayer. Maimonides makes this explicit. After stating the requirement of concentration as a prerequisite to acceptable prayer, he writes: "What is meant by concentration? Every prayer which lacks concentration is not prayer. . . . What is concentration? A man must remove from his heart all thoughts and see himself as standing in God's presence."[12] The attitude required here is emotional and subjective; it has to do with inner feeling rather than external conduct. Similarly, the Mishnah requires, by way of exhibiting love for God, that an individual bless God on the occasion of evil even as he blesses God when he is the recipient of a good.[13] The Talmud also makes it clear that "to bless" means to rejoice.[14]

Further, the very same feeling may receive both a subjective and an objective interpretation in rabbinic commentary. Consider the obligation to love God. Maimonides names one of the fourteen books that comprise his code of Jewish law "The Book of Love." This book, which defines in practical, behavioral terms the meaning of the love of the Supreme Being, treats of the laws that deal with the recitation of the Shema and the Amidah, the use of tefillin, mezuzah, and a Sefer Torah, the tzitzit on the four-cornered garment, the variety of blessings recited by a Jew in different circumstances, and circumcision. In sum, the book deals with the subjective sentiment of love and the way it is objectified in visible public practice. On the other hand, when Maimonides describes the love of God in "The Book of Knowledge," which is also included in his Code, he writes: "When a man looks at His great and marvelous works and creations, and notes in them His wisdom, which is of infinite and endless value, immediately he loves and praises and extols and experiences a great desire to know His great name."[15] Here, Maimonides utilizes subjective terms ("love," "desire") in his account of the love of God. It is clear that according to this account, both aspects, the subjective and the objective, are essential to the process of religious expression from the halakhic standpoint.

Rabbi Soloveitchik also gave expression, and in dramatic form, to both elements. While the objective component is the focus of his *Halakhic Man*, the subjective dimension receives elaborate attention in his later works, *The Lonely Man of Faith* and more recently, *Uvikashtem Misham*. In these works, which underscore subjectivity, there is, for example, the following passage:

> The role of the man of faith, whose religious experience is fraught with inner conflicts and incongruities, who oscillates between ecstasy in God's companionship and despair when he feels abandoned by God, and who is torn asunder by the heightened contrast between self-appreciation and self-abnegation, has been a difficult one since the times of Abraham and Moses. It would be presumptuous of me to attempt to convert the passional, antinomic faith-experience into a

eudaemonic, harmonious one, while the biblical knights of faith lived heroically with this very tragic and paradoxical experience.[16]

How, then, is the relationship between subjective and objective, between passion and action, to be described? The answer appears to be that both are important, that there is an organic relationship between them, but that primacy is to be assigned to the objective component.

The claim that there is an organic relation between the two should be understood in the following sense: two entities may be said to be organically related if they are mutually cause-and-effect of each other, i.e., each is a cause of the other, and each is impacted by the other. Within our context, it means that a stronger emotion will be translated into actions that are more meaningful (e.g., the greater the love of God, the more concentration and focus will be available in prayer), and that repeated actions will enhance the sentiments which should be the appropriate subjective correlative to these actions (when a person recites the Shema and Amidah daily, it strengthens his sense of involvement with the Divine Being).

The objective component, in the halakhic point of view, is nevertheless paramount. Judaism's theological foundation consists, not of the thirteen principles of faith, no matter how important they may be, but of the six hundred and thirteen commandments. Judaism is primarily a religion of the covenant, and its major category is the mitzvah.

9

Halakhah and Science

A generally accepted contemporary interpretation of the nature of scientific theory is that it is a theoretical construction, an imaginative creation, an *a priori* system useful for the explanation of a universe of facts. The point of this claim is that the theory does not describe structure inherent in the universe; it is rather a heuristic device for the explanation of phenomenon and prediction of events. It is a theoretical system, the creation, rather than the discovery, of a great scientist, imposed on a universe of facts which fortunately lend themselves to successful explanation by the theory.

A great philosopher of science, for example, maintained that ideal entities of physics, e.g., the instantaneous velocity of Mars, refer to nothing that exists in the universe, notwithstanding the fact that such notions are indispensable in the explication of gravitational theory.

> It is difficult to interpret expressions which assign real number values to the magnitudes of physical properties as signifying empirically identifiable traits in the explicit subject matter of physics. . . . In using real number expressions to denote the instantaneous velocity of Mars at any given time, we are . . . predicating something of Mars which, on the basis of the ordinary use of the term "velocity," it could not possibly have. The expression "the instantaneous velocity of Mars" thus seems to denote nothing in the heavens.[1]

It should be noted that the concept of theoretical construction is utilized even in giving an account of the nature of matter. As another celebrated philosopher maintained, "Whenever possible, logical constructions are to be substituted for inferred entities."[2] He argued that the idea of a material object is not inferred from, but theoretically constructed out of, the experience of sense data.

Rabbi Joseph B. Soloveitchik elaborates on this scientific thesis.

The latter approach is that of mathematics and the mathematical natural sciences, the crowning achievement of civilization. It is both *a priori* and ideal—i.e. to know means to construct an ideal, lawful, unified system whose necessity flows from its very nature, a system that does not require, as far as its validity and truth are concerned, precise parallelism with the correlative realm of concrete, qualitative phenomena. On the contrary all that we have is an approximate accord. . . . There exists an ideal world and a concrete one, and between the two only an approximate parallelism prevails.[3]

Rabbi Soloveitchik then utilized this idea to give an account of halakhah. He maintained that halakhah is also an *a priori* system, a theoretical construction, that is imposed on experience.

When halakhic man approaches reality, he comes with the Torah given him from Sinai, in hand. He orients himself to the world by means of fixed statutes and firm principles. An entire corpus of precepts and laws guides him along the path leading to existence. Halakhic man, well furnished with rules, judgments and fundamental principles, draws near the world with an *a priori* relation. His approach begins with an ideal creation and concludes with a real one. To whom may he be compared? To a mathematician who fashions an ideal world and uses it for the purpose of establishing a relation between it and the real world.[4]

An ideal creation in the halakhic domain is a set of *a priori* precepts which, when placed in relation to the realm of experience, or better still, when imposed on that realm, results in a world that embodies value.

I

On this approach, values are placed in the same category as the theoretical entities of physics. The latter e.g., the electron or the electromagnetic wave, entities denoted by theoretical terms, are not values and do not prescribe conduct. They belong to the category of thing, though it is not assumed that instances of these things are exemplified in the nonmental universe. The halakhah, on the other hand, is a value system which presupposes normative ideals which it translates into rules of conduct. Both values and the theoretical terms of physics are *a priori* in the sense that they are imposed, not discovered, in the experienced world.

Scientists do not require that theoretical entities reproduce in theory structure that is contained in the real world. Instead, they interpret such entities and the scientific theories of which they are constituents as models.[5] When a scientist proposes a model, he is in effect declaring that *if* the structure of the universe were identical to that of the model, our experience of the world would be precisely what it is in fact. But he does not maintain that the model precisely reflects existing reality. If it is possible to infer from the theory in which the theoretical terms are embedded laws that can be used successfully in the task of explaining and predicting phenomena in the experienced universe, then there exists a certain harmony between theory and fact that makes the theoretical terms useful to the enterprise of science.

It is not necessary to argue at length that halakhic values do not inhere in the universe. If the halakhah declares that the day which arrives at sunset Friday has the sanctity of the Sabbath day, the intent is not that the period from sundown on Friday to sundown on Saturday, as a physical span of time, has a character which another day, say sundown Monday to sundown Tuesday, does not have. As physical entities, they are identical and indistinguishable. The value of sanctity does not reflect any inherent subject matter; its source is *a priori*.

II

In science, a distinction can be made between an ideal entity and one that is purely theoretical. An ideal entity is present in nature, though not in pure form; a theoretical entity may not exist in nature at all. An example of the former is Newton's law of inertia. It declares that a body on which no force is acting, if at rest, remains at rest, and if in motion, continues in uniform motion in a straight line. But there is no body in nature which is removed from the influence of all forces whatsoever. Bodies, however, could be arranged in a declining order in which those further in the sequence are under the influence of weaker forces. One can then extrapolate, after studying the behavior of the bodies in the sequence, and infer the behavior of a body, if such existed, under the influence of no force whatsoever. As a matter of fact, however, there is no body that is free of all forces; such a body is an ideal entity.

A theoretical entity, on the other hand, is not one that differs in degree from an actually existing body; it is, instead, one that scientists are willing to grant is entirely *a priori* and unexemplified in the entire realm of nature. The introduction of the concept of the electromagnetic wave is a practical device invented for the purpose of facilitating the task of explanation and prediction. The most that scientists would say is that light behaves *as if* it consisted of waves of a certain kind, but they do not claim that a counterpart of the theoretical notion of the electromagnetic wave is to be found in nature.

A halakhic value, however, has both these characteristics, i.e., it is ideal *and* theoretical. In the first place, it is theoretical. Values do not mix well with facts, which is to say that they are not inherent aspects of objects in nature. To be good or just is not in the same category as being blue or hot. The latter traits *belong* to objects; values are judgments that we *associate* with objects, i.e., they are theoretical and *a priori*.

In addition, they are ideal. Even when attached, let us say, to an action, a value is not perfectly embodied in that action. Consider piety by way of example. This religious value is normally defined in terms of the recitation of prayers, the contemplation of prescribed thoughts, the adoption of recommended psychological states, such as a sense of intimacy with the Divine Being. It is obvious that, at best, this religious value is exemplified only to a degree in individual expressions of piety. It is in the same category as a body on which no force is acting. No instance of either exists. No matter how much enthusiasm an individual may generate in prayer or some other act of piety, it could be maintained that he has not attained its perfect state. Piety, in its ideal form, is nowhere to be found.

III

There is, of course, this difference between halakhah and science: in science, the *a priori* must submit to facts; in halakhah, the facts must submit to the *a priori*. In science, the empirical fact is the court of last resort. If the proposition which formulates the fact is incompatible with some proposition logically implied by the theory which is intended to explain the empirical domain to which the fact belongs, then the theory must be modified or discarded. The results of the Michaelson-Morley experiment revealed a flaw in the theoretical apparatus of science. This led to the reformulation of the theory of gravity in Einstein's theory of relativity. If a theory is not in consonance with the facts to which it is relevant, the theory must undergo transformation.

In the halakhic perspective, on the other hand, the fact must accommodate itself to the value. In truth, values cannot be inconsistent with facts, i.e., values and facts cannot stand in contradiction. David Hume argued, as is well known among those who engage in philosophic discourse, that an "ought" statement cannot be deduced from an "is" proposition. An "ought" statement asserts an obligation; an "is" statement describes a state of affairs. These are logically independent of each other.[6] Nevertheless, when we consider the facts of human behavior, we discover that values are often associated with facts. For example, the statistical fact that a large segment of society engages in premarital cohabitation is taken by many as tantamount to the assertion that such activity is good, i.e., possesses value. Accordingly, a more accurate statement of the case is that, in the halakhic perspective, the value associated with the fact must accommodate itself to the value of halakhah. The goal is invariably that of transforming the fact so that the value associated with it shall be entirely consistent with halakhic norms. Hence, if for example the halakhah projects as a value the sanctity of the marriage bond, which implies that adulterous relations are proscribed, then although as a matter of sociological fact adultery may be rampant in the community, it is not the halakhic value but the fact that must submit to change.

This point needs to be stressed particularly in the context of Jewish life. The fundamental basis of Judaism is not so much the belief as the precept of action. Its central focus is not essentially the principles of faith but the imperatives of behavior. It is principally this circumstance that has prompted the judgment that Judaism is this-worldly rather than other-worldly. The judgment is sound, but it must be correctly understood. The priority that Judaism assigns to halakhic values over values associated with facts means that the this-worldly character of Judaism is not expressed in submission to this world (of fact), but in a preoccupation to transform it so that it shall be in accord with the world of norms articulated by the halakhah.

IV

The priority of the halakhic *a priori* over empirical facts is manifested not only in the denigration of fact in relation to halakhic value, but also in the circumstance that the fact is often ignored, even denied, in order to realize the value.

A prime example of this halakhic tendency is a description by Nachmanides of what is required in the posture of humility. In a letter to his son, he writes, "Let every man be greater than you in your eyes."[7] Now it is clear that, as a matter of fact, it is not the case that every man is greater than the humble person, no matter what standard of greatness is adopted. The facts, however, are in this instance to be ignored. The obligation to be humble requires the adoption of an attitude incompatible with the facts.

A corollary of the precept of humility is the Jewish view on equality. In Judaism, this principle is prescriptive rather than descriptive. The halakhah does not declare that all men are equal as a matter of fact. Such a claim, given our experience, is clearly untenable. The most that can be said about the principle of equality is that it is prescriptive, i.e., notwithstanding the facts to the contrary, and at the very least (for according to Nachmanides we ought to perceive others as superior to ourselves), we are to regard and treat all human beings as equals.

The arrival of a new lunar month has crucial halakhic consequences. The identification of a day as the first day of Tishri implies that the festival of Rosh Hashanah is to be celebrated on that day, and that ten days hence, on Yom Kippur, there is an obligation to fast. But it is not the fact of the appearance of the new moon that determines when the month of Tishri begins, but the declaration of a competent court convened for that purpose. If the court decides that the month shall begin the following day, then notwithstanding the appearance of the moon on the preceding day, Rosh Hashanah is celebrated on the day designated by the court.

Accordingly, the halakhic personality elevates himself above facts, to create a world in his imagination controlled by halakhic precepts and to respond to the *a priori* rather than to the empirical fact in determining the course of his life.

V

The halakhah's emphasis on the theoretical is exhibited in its judgment that its values are imposed rather than discovered in facts, in that it strives to achieve consistency between its norms and the values associated with facts by transforming the facts if they fail to exemplify the norms, and by requiring, in many instances, that halakhic persons live in a world of imagination where even that which is imagined is incompatible with facts. The halakhah, even more than science, gives priority to the *a priori*.

10

A This-Worldly Religion

It is an ancient insight that Judaism is this-worldly. This suggests an unique conception of the relation between the spiritual world of the Divine Being and the natural universe of the human being, between the city of God and the city of man—one that differs radically from views entertained by other religions. It needs to be stressed, in view of the fact that Judaism is sometimes erroneously deprecated on the grounds that it advocates total immersion in the material and the hedonistic, that the claim that Judaism is this-worldly is an assertion concerning the *spiritual* dimension of Jewish life. It merely directs attention to Judaism's conception of the locus of the spiritual. It in effect declares that the domain of the spiritual is not to be found exclusively in the realm of the transcendent. Insofar as man is concerned, it may be located and, in addition, needs to be introduced on earth.

I

One feature of Judaism's this-worldly character is that it adopts a positive attitude to the things of this world. It rejects any suggestion to the effect that a vast and unbridgeable chasm separates the realm of the spiritual from the material. On the contrary, they are perceived as intimately intertwined.

Judaism adopts a version of the well-known philosophic doctrine of dualism that differs significantly from that of other religions. This doctrine has both a metaphysical and a moral interpretation. Metaphysically it means that the universe consists of two distinctive and contrasting types of elements; one is body, and the other spirit. As the philosophers put it, the attribute of one is extension and that of the other is thought, i.e., they have nothing in common. The same metaphysical dualism, it is claimed, characterizes the human being. He consists of a material body and a soul that belongs to the domain of spirit. But in saying that the two components of man and the universe are radically different, no claim is made concerning the value of either. The same dualism would exist if matter and spirit were judged to be value-neutral or of equal value. At this point, a moral dualism is introduced which asserts that the realm of the spirit is good and that of the body is evil. The source of this doctrine is ancient, introduced in a philosophic dialogue in which we are informed that the philosopher looks forward to the release of the soul from the prison of the body.[1] This view was appropriated by the religions of Western civilization. Judaism endorses the doctrine of metaphysical dualism, but rejects the notion that it has as a counterpart a moral dualism. The two sets of categories—soul and body, on the one hand, and good and evil, on the other—are not coextensive

God created the world and "He saw that it was good." This refers to the created, physical universe. It applies to man as well. One might object that, even on the Jewish view, there is an evil element in the human psychological anatomy. We speak of both *yetzer hatov*, the good inclination, and *yetzer hara*, the evil inclination. The former is often associated with spiritual characteristics, such as reason, knowledge and wisdom, functions of the soul, and the latter with emotions and impulses that have their seat in the body. This seems to imply that activities of the soul are good and those of the body evil, but such a view is not in accord with Jewish conceptions. There is, for example, a midrashic commentary based on a verse toward the conclusion of the biblical creation chapter, "and God saw all that He had done, and behold it was very good," to the effect that God saw it was good" refers to the good inclination, while "God saw it was very good" refers to the evil inclination.[2] The Midrash explains that were it not for the evil inclination, man would not build houses, plant trees, engage in business, and get married. Accordingly, it is the so-called evil inclination that provides the impulse, the urge, and the motivation to undertake initiatives that will assure the fulfillment of the divine command of *vekhivshuha*, "you shall conquer the universe." The allegedly evil inclination turns out to be not evil at all. It may indeed, on occasion, prod the human being to acts that are evil, but it is also the source of creativity and of great moral achievements. One could argue that when impulse—hatred, for example—places reason in its service, as when the Nazis utilized science to implement their diabolical Final Solution, reason itself became corrupt and demonic. Good and evil cannot, in Jewish thought, be made to correspond to soul and body, i.e., to reason and emotion. Their contours do not coincide.

There is the talmudic doctrine of resurrection of the human being, i.e., the ultimate restoration of a reunited body and soul. This is obviously to be distinguished from the tenet which affirms the immortality of the soul. A religious view that accepts the Platonic claim that the soul is the prisoner of the body would be comfortable with a dogma of immortality but would not allow one of resurrection. Why restore to existence in the end of days something that is inherently evil? But for Judaism evil is not an inevitable characteristic of the body, so the doctrine of resurrection can be, and indeed is, central to its creed.

Jewish thinkers have noted that the body is the essential focus of the mitzvot. The purpose of the commandments is to train impulses and fashion responses in such a way that bodily actions will coincide with Torah precepts. Such an interpretation of the primary objectives of Torah law suggests that there is no chasm separating body from soul. Some religions are concerned exclusively with the soul; their goal is to introduce maximum distance between soul and body. Their objective is not to shape impulse but to deny and frustrate it. Judaism seeks to mold impulse through the practice of Torah precepts.

We may take this a step further. The goal of the commandments is not merely to habituate the body to act in a manner that exemplifies that which is good; it is more. Its aim is to sanctify the body. This is accomplished by taking physical impulses, even those as basic as hunger and erotic desire, and attaching to their expression the performance of mitzvot. We do not merely eat to slake our hunger. On Shabbat, for example, we eat to fulfill the halakhic obligation of partaking of three meals by way of celebrating this sacred day. The satisfaction of biological impulses of the romantic variety is also associated with the fulfillment of halakhic imperatives in order to elevate, ennoble, indeed to sanctify them

Clearly, this is a radically different approach. To aspire to holiness, one does not merely engage in prayer, fasting, and acts of contrition and penitence. Rather, one pursues fulfillment for the biological organism, but does so in the process of appropriating spiritual values prescribed by Torah. These values are intended to give character and quality to patterns of conduct that are normal for the human species—marriage, procreation, educating the members of the family, building the institutions that will preserve and enhance human experience and Jewish life.

The rabbis teach that "a sage who dies is like a Torah scroll that was burned."[3] The body, accordingly, bereft of its soul, retains sanctity. It was the body that was essentially involved in the performance of mitzvot—refraining from work on the Sabbath, putting on tefillin and wrapping itself in a tallit, eating matzah, shaking the lulav, fasting on Yom Kippur, etc. In preparation for burial, the physical remains of a human being are handled with respect and reverence, for they are sacred.

II

The this-worldliness of Judaism is also made manifest through its emphasis on law. Judaism is primarily a religion of law rather than belief. Among the faiths of Western civilization, belief focuses on doctrines concerning God and His relation to the universe. The theological axiom is that if one believes correctly, he will be saved. Salvation is a function of correctness in belief. The religion of law is covenantal in character. It requires not correct opinion so much as correct action. Not all rabbinic thinkers agreed with Maimonides that a genuinely Jewish religious posture demands a knowledge of the attributes of God (to the extent, of course, that they can be known).[4] What is necessary is an acceptance of the obligations that were covenantally agreed upon at Sinai. Those obligations translate into law.

If one accepts the law as Judaism's essential feature, it is not difficult to make the case that it is this-worldly. This is obviously so with respect to the imperatives that prescribe man's relation to fellow man. The result of adhering to these precepts is to ensure constructive human relationships in accordance with moral and spiritual criteria. But it has been maintained that this is also true of the precepts that require specified behavior in relation to the Almighty. Rabbi Soloveitchik has argued that unlike other religions, which seek to elevate man to heaven, Judaism seeks to bring God down to man.[5] By obedience to halakhic precepts, the human being and members of society cultivate not only a moral but a religious character, enabling them to sense the presence of God in human affairs. Rabbi Samson R. Hirsch argued along different lines, though with the same net result, that the Torah was not intended as a springboard to enable us to discover truths about God, but rather as an expression of that which God wants of men on earth.[6] In either case, Judaism evinces itself to be this-worldly even in respect to those precepts that guide our conduct in relation to the Supreme Being.

A this-worldly orientation with a concomitant emphasis on law assigns special importance to moral precepts because they are perceived as belonging to a domain not at all removed from the religious and spiritual. An other-worldly theological view could sever the two. Even while it would assign importance to moral behavior, it could perceive such conduct as belonging essentially to the city of man rather than the city of God. In any case, conduct in relation to God, in the form of belief, prayer, and abstinence, would carry greater spiritual weight. On a this-worldly view, according to which the city of God includes the city of man, moral precepts take on supreme theological significance, for they are no less the word of God than those that are distinctively precepts "between man and God." They are at least on the same level and in some ways may be even more important. The rabbis describe the transgressions of the generation of Noah which resulted in the deluge as consisting of idolatry, adultery and incest, and violence toward fellow men. Based on a careful examination of the text, they conclude that the flood was exclusively a consequence of violence and not at all an effect of the other egregious sins.[7] Redemption of the social variety is clearly impossible so long as the members of society aggressively invade each other's rights to life and property.

It is not surprising, therefore, that Judaism provides guidance with respect to every arena of human life. An other-worldly religion would focus its concerns primarily upon those doctrines and sacraments that are essential for salvation, a concept that is interpreted in terms of life in the heaven of the spirit. A this-worldly religion must concern itself with every phase of human life, for its primary objective is to mold a society that will embody, in its conduct and demeanor, spiritual values relevant to life here and now.

It may be fairly concluded that while a religion of belief is oriented toward assuring for its followers the blessing of salvation in the world to come, a this-worldly religion has an orientation more in line with the path leading to redemption, which is understood as a successful and fulfilling life on earth in the context of an entire community in accordance with the will of God. Jews always pray for and await the realization of the ge'ulah aharonah, the final redemption, which is to arrive in the era of the Messiah. The rabbis explain that on that day, "the world will continue on its usual course."[8] No change in the natural order of things will occur. What will happen is that the sovereignty of the house of David will be restored, the Holy Temple will be rebuilt, and the entire house of Israel will be returned to its homeland. Redemption is clearly a this-worldly state of affairs.

Law enhances the respect of human beings for each other and contributes to the processes leading to redemption. Normally, at least in a democratic context, law is understood as essential to prevent one citizen from interfering with the rights of another. On this approach, law is of interest primarily to lawyers, jurists, and those who are accused of violating it. Judaism however interprets the law primarily in terms of its pedagogic value. It is therefore taught, in the form of Talmud study, in the classroom, to children who are relatively young. The Talmud also declares that there are laws in the

Torah which will never be implemented. In its words and by way of illustration, "The law of the rebellious son never found application and never will."[9] The implications are that it is contrary to human nature that this law, given the biblical conditions for its use, could ever find exemplification. It is nevertheless included among the biblical imperatives to teach a Jew certain values, to mold his conscience in such a way that it will reflect the moral and humane. In short, the essential purpose of law is education for a moral and religious life. If this were accomplished for all members of society, the process of redemption would be advanced.

Redemption has an existential, i.e., an individual, as well as a social form. But even its existential variety is of a this-worldly character. It is defined, not in terms of an ascension to a heavenly abode, but in terms of a life here and now which experiences a sense of self-worth because of an awareness of a relationship with the Supreme Being. This relationship derives from adhering to the will of the Supreme Being as expressed in the mitzvot of Torah. Of course, classical Judaism interprets existential redemption in terms of life in the hereafter as well. The point, however, is that its focus is primarily on existential redemption in the present.

It should be added that the idea of salvation is also a this-worldly concept for Judaism. Salvation is what the Jewish people was granted when it was emancipated from its slavery in Egypt and what every Jew prays for when he finds himself in the straits. The idea of salvation is not perceived as part of the doctrine of immortality, nor is it essential to it. Salvation is something a Jew needs on occasion in the present world, i.e., when his life or that of his community is threatened and he finds himself incapable of doing anything about it.

III

Because Judaism is this-worldly, it is concerned, not only with morality, but with ethics. Morality deals with principles guiding man's relation to man. Ethics, in its classic sense, is concerned with the question of human happiness. The ancient Greeks put the question baldly: what must one do to achieve happiness?

Judaism answers that happiness includes satisfactions enjoyed in the present life in connection with the performing of mitzvot. There are three Hebrew terms that refer to the experience of pleasure: *hana'ah*, physical pleasure; *simḥah*, joy; *oneg*, spiritual delight. Physical pleasure in itself is not assigned inherent value, though it enters on occasion into halakhic discussion. It is a crucial component, for example, in the definition of eating. By way of illustration, a prohibition exists requiring that we refrain from certain foods (e.g., meat of nonkosher animals), but the consumption of tasteless or bitter morsels is not "eating" according to the halakhic definition.[10] No spiritual value, however, is assigned to such pleasures. The sheer stimulation of the sense organs for the sake of a hedonistic experience is not encouraged, though it is permitted within limits. The experience of pleasure does receive halakhic endorsement when it is combined with the performance of mitzvot, in which circumstances the pleasure is itself spiritualized. It is a pleasure which enhances the satisfaction of the performance of the mitzvah.

Spiritualized pleasure, however, takes two forms; one is *simḥah*, and the other *oneg*. *Simḥah*, joy, is prescribed in connection with the celebration of festivals. The rabbinic principle enunciated with regard to such celebrations is *ḥetzia lashem veḥetzia lakhem*, "half of your celebration should be directed to God and half to yourself."[11] Maimonides explains:

> In the morning, all the people rise and go to the synagogues and halls of study. They pray and read in the Torah concerning the festival day. Then they return to their homes to eat, following which they proceed to the study halls for study until midday. They then recite the Minḥah service and return to their homes to eat and drink for the remainder of the day. When a man eats and drinks and rejoices during the festival, he should avoid too much wine and refrain from jesting and irreverent behavior, for this is not joy but confusion and foolishness.[12]

According to Maimonides, not all pleasures are suited to the human portion. One should indulge oneself only with those which, according to biblical prescription, are part of the celebration of the festival. Rashi adds that by eating and drinking, the Jew demonstrates that he is pleased with that part of the Jewish heritage which is the cause of the celebration, such as the Torah on Shavuot.[13]

Oneg is an experience where the material is spiritualized to an even higher degree. *Oneg* is appropriate to the Sabbath, just as *simḥah* is applicable to the festival. One of the ways in which the spiritualization of the Shabbat exceeds that of the festival is the singing of *zemirot*. These are not merely songs of any kind, for songs are also appropriate for a festival. *Zemirot* are songs in honor of God and the Sabbath day. The introduction of these melodies at the Sabbath meal enhances its spiritual quality.

In a general way, it should be noted that not all pleasures are the same. There are pleasures, pure and simple, of the animal or psychological variety. But pleasures attached to the performance of mitzvot do not merely enhance the experience of fulfilling the will of God, they are themselves modified and enriched by the association. The intent is not merely a matter of attaining simultaneity, i.e., of performing a mitzvah and at the same time and independently enjoying pleasures. The aim is rather to introduce an organic relation between the two, to transform pleasures in such a way that they become something distinctive and unique because of the association. The situation is entirely analogous to the understanding of a language. When we listen to discourse in a strange language before we understand the meanings of the words, we hear jumbled sounds. As soon as we learn the meanings, the very same sounds are heard differently, even though they are enunciated identically by the speaker. The experience of hearing is transformed by infusing sounds with meaning. Analogously, the experience of pleasure is modified when it is infused with spiritual meaning. When the latter occurs, to one degree or another, we have *simḥah* or *oneg*.

The phrase in Isaiah is *vekarata lashabbat oneg*, "you shall call the Sabbath a delight."[14] In rabbinic interpretation, to call something by a name is to express one of its attributes. For the prophet, delight is a name of the Sabbath day, irrespective of the food that is eaten by way of celebrating it. And though partaking of three meals is an expression of *oneg*, the thrust is not to satisfy culinary taste or to appease hunger but to deepen and intensify the spiritual significance of the day. The point is that the activity of eating on the Sabbath should itself be a spiritual event. *Simḥah* does not require the transformation of the physical to the same extent. But whether the experience is one of *simḥah* or *oneg*, it is this-worldly in character; the delight that is the Sabbath day, at least in the here and now, is this-worldly.

IV

Perhaps the best manifestation of the this-worldly nature of Judaism is its incorporation of a land, the land of Israel, into the scheme of its spiritual life. The land is central to Jewish religious life, as shown by the number of biblical imperatives that depend for their fulfillment on its possession. These imperatives—*mitzvot hateluyyot ba'aretz*, "commandments that are dependent on the land"—are primarily directed at agricultural elements of life in Israel. They are concerned with the distribution of portions of the harvest to the priest, the levite, and the indigent, with the obligation for the farmer to present his first fruits to the priest, with the requirement that land be allowed to remain fallow every seventh year, etc. The land and its laws belong to the material domain, the this-worldly realm of human concerns.

But the land presupposes this-worldliness in other ways as well, for the concept of land does not merely connote the rocks and earth that constitute the soil of Israel. Indeed, it is meaningless to speak of a land of Israel, i.e., a land belonging to the people of Israel, unless a government of the people of Israel exists with rights of ownership with respect to the entire land. If every piece of the land belonged to Jews but the land were under the sovereignty of an alien power, it could not be regarded as the land of Israel. Implicit, therefore, in the concept of the land of Israel is a Jewish sovereign power which exercises control over the entire geographic area that is the land of Israel.[15]

In point of fact, the Book of Deuteronomy makes clear what the idea of the land of Israel entails. It speaks of the designation of a sovereign to organize the social and political relations of its inhabitants and to defend them, especially against the Amalekites, the historic enemies of our people; it requires the organization of a Sanhedrin, the supreme legislative and judicial body, as well as a system of courts to administer justice; it defines social patterns of conduct, with special emphasis on deviant relations between man and woman, child and parents, and so on. All the functions of a state described in this book are essential to the possession of the land, and all of them are this-worldly concerns.

Obviously, one cannot have a society that devotes itself exclusively to spiritual matters, such as praying, fasting, and doing penance on an ongoing basis, and expect its communal life to be arranged in a satisfactory way. The members of society must involve themselves in the normal occupations that are characteristic of the world here and now in order for the society in which they live to remain strong and viable. It is clear that to allow a geographic area to become central to the religious experience is inevitably to insist on a this-worldly perspective.

But the notion of the land with its concomitant idea of the state directs attention to still another this-worldly feature of Judaism as a religion, namely, a positive attitude toward power. Power is substantially irrelevant to an other-worldly perspective. If the religious goal is exclusively spiritual, i.e., other-worldly, then asceticism is often encouraged and suffering regarded as elevating and ennobling, leading to the goal of spiritual salvation. In such a perspective, power should be—though it is not always—eschewed as not merely irrelevant but detrimental to the spiritual objective. When, however, the religious goal is not other-worldly salvation but this-worldly redemption, and redemption is interpreted in terms of creating a society which embodies Torah values in ideal form, then power as an instrument facilitating the achievement of the religious goal may well be construed as indispensable. So the Torah prescribes it as a mitzvah that the people of Israel designate a sovereign who will utilize the power available in political organization to assist in achieving Israel's redemptive ends.

Political power is the greatest source of power, for it includes many of the other varieties, such as economic, military, and technological power. The Bible also commands the human species to conquer the universe, *vekhivshuha*, an imperative which Rabbi Joseph B. Soloveitchik interprets in terms of technology and Rabbi Samson R. Hirsch in terms of material accumulations. Both, however, affirm the value of power—one in the form of scientific creativity, and the other in its economic variety—in the enterprise of realizing God's purposes on earth. This is a clear and explicit statement of the importance of power in a this-worldly perspective.

V

In sum, the idea that Judaism is a this-worldly religion encompasses a variety of components, each of which is essential to the very definition of Jewish life. It includes a positive attitude toward the physical universe; an emphasis on the religious significance of moral, as distinguished from purely spiritual, conduct; an acceptance of the ingredient of joy in human experience; and equally an affirmation of the value of power.

11

Religion and Politics

One might suppose that the relation between religion and politics parallels that between religion and culture. It is clear from the preceding discussions that there are two ways of viewing culture, one from the standpoint of *Torah umadda*, and the other from that of *Torah im derekh eretz*. There is a much more intimate relationship between the two in the perspective of *Torah im derekh eretz* than there is in that of *Torah umadda*. The latter regards religion and culture as totally independent of each other. It recognizes that there are biblically prescribed mandates to pursue both, but it keeps them apart. It merely requires of an individual that he become involved with both. *Torah im derekh eretz*, on the other hand, perceives religion and culture as intertwined, both constituents of Torah.[1]

One might be inclined to extrapolate from this analysis to the relationship between religion and politics. On the view of *Torah umadda*, the two would belong to entirely different realms, and according to the doctrine of *Torah im derekh eretz*, the political enterprise would be regarded as an essential component of Torah. This, however, is not a satisfactory way of stating the case, because unlike the model of Torah and culture, whose relationship is not explicitly addressed in the Torah, the relation between Torah and the political realm receives detailed definition in the sacred texts. In the Book of Deuteronomy, we are informed that the biblically sanctioned sovereign has religious functions. Among other things, he must carry a Torah scroll at all times.[2] According to the Mishnah, the king was required to read the Torah to the community of Israel once every seven years in the Holy Temple.[3] The only acceptable standpoint is that which can be expressed in the phrase *Torah im medinah*, i.e., the state has halakhic status.

But what is the nature of the endorsement that the halakhah grants the state? It is not enough to say that the biblical passage *authorizes* the establishment of a temporal power on earth to run the affairs of state. While an authorization of this kind would represent one form of approbation, it does not imply that the state thereby acquires halakhic status. On the view of *Torah umadda*, for example, there is a biblical mandate for the Jew to become involved in the study and acquisition of culture (for according to Rabbi Joseph B. Soloveitchik, as has already been noted, this is the meaning of *vekhivshuha*, "you shall exercise control over the universe"),[4] but this authorization does not justify the conclusion that culture is assigned halakhic status, because on this view, the study of cultural matters is not held to be among the mitzvot of Torah.[5] Neither need culture be perceived as a mitzvah according to the view of *Torah im derekh eretz*, which, while it declares that culture is part of Torah, may not place it in the category of a Torah precept. It is otherwise with the command to appoint a monarch. This precept is universally acknowledged to be in the category of a mitzvah, however the mandate to establish a sovereign power may be defined.

There is a dispute in the Talmud as to whether the Torah merely allows the designation of a king or categorically requires it. The amora Samuel argued that the chapter on the sovereign in Deuteronomy 17 mandates the establishment of a monarchy, while according to Rav, his talmudic adversary, the biblical passage in question merely teaches appropriate behavior toward a monarch if one is designated, though (as Rashi observes in his interpretation of Rav's comment) it is desirable to avoid the institution altogether.[6] On one view, therefore, the Torah did not advocate the creation of this institution. It was only a concession in anticipation of the inevitable demands of human nature. There was a divine expectation that the people of Israel would insist on a monarch, and biblical provision was made. On the other view, the Torah requires the designation of a sovereign. According to this interpretation, it would appear that a sovereign is perceived to be an essential component in the distinctively religious landscape and necessary for the achievement of the divine purpose on earth. However, even if the institution of the sovereign is merely permitted—perhaps the hesitation to give him wholehearted endorsement is rooted in a suspicion that the power inevitably concentrated in his hands may turn him away from the Torah and its imperatives—this does not deprive him of the status of one whose position and function is biblically mandated as a mitzvah.[7]

Further, the mitzvah with respect to the designation of a sovereign is concerned exclusively with the kind of state the people of Israel should have; it does not address the prior question as to whether a Jewish state should be created. The latter is dealt with, at least implicitly, in the chapter of the Torah which describes the *berit bein habetarim*, the Covenant among the Parts. God said to Abraham, "To your descendants have I given this land."[8] This means that the land is to belong to the Jewish people. The circumstances in which this claim could be made have already been described.[9] If the land were under the sovereignty of a strange and alien power, it could not be identified as the land of Israel even if every inch of it were occupied by a Jew. If the people of Israel, on the other hand, are sovereign in the land, it would be identified as the land of Israel even if strangers were in possession of large tracts of its territory. Implicit, therefore, in God's promise to give the land to the descendants of Abraham is that a Jewish state will exist.

The state could take a variety of forms. It could be a loose, decentralized confederation of relatively independent tribes, as was the case until Saul became king of ancient Israel, or it could take the centralized form of a monarchy. The chapter concerning the king merely prescribes a form of government for a state whose existence had already heretofore been mandated.

It is clear, therefore, that the obligation to establish a Jewish state is not only affirmed explicitly in one of the mitzvot of Torah; it is also the result of a covenant drawn between God and Abraham which promised the holy land to the descendants of the patriarch. In these senses, the Jewish state has both halakhic sanction and covenantal endorsement.

I

But can a state which is organized according to principles antithetical to halakhah possess halakhic sanction? The problem arises today; it existed in ancient days as well.

It should be noted in the first place that in talmudic discussions, the creation of a sovereign power is intimately related to two disparate goals—one, to do battle against Amalek, i.e., to, ensure the preservation of the security of the Jewish community; the other, the building of the Holy Temple. The Talmud declares that these three mandates, to wit, designating a monarch, doing battle against the enemy, and building the House of God, are to occur in a certain temporal and logical sequence. First the sovereign is appointed; then the enemy is defeated; finally the Temple is built.[10] It follows that the monarch is confronted with a twofold task. One is secular—that of *tikkun haolam*, the preservation and well-being of the community, an assignment which is generally understood in human terms. The monarch must be creative in devising ways and means of utilizing all the resources that the state makes available to enhance the security of the society with whose well-being he is charged. The other is spiritual—the creation of the central institution of communal worship, the building of a religious community focused on the study and practice of Torah and worship in the Holy Temple. Both tasks are important, but the question of priority remains. The issue is not which of the two goals of the sovereign is the more important; it is rather: with which is he principally charged?

In his religious function, the monarch may be regarded as a representative of the Almighty; in his secular assignment, he would be perceived as serving the community. If the emphasis is placed on the former, his conduct would not only be expected to be entirely in accord with religious precepts, but the tolerance of the religious community would be severely strained if the sovereign failed to discharge his religious as well as his political obligations fully. If the focus is on the latter, his deviations and foibles could be more readily tolerated, because while he is by biblical prescription required to abide by Torah and to support it, he would be perceived as one whose primary responsibility is ensuring the defense and security of his people. Because, as a matter of historical fact, the behavior of the sovereign, more often than not, was at variance with the requirements of Torah, the tendency emerged to see him in terms of his secular function, which involves primarily the defense of the community.

The problem is not novel; it existed in ancient times as well. The sovereign who is assigned a dual function by the halakhah takes only one of them seriously—the secular one. In ancient days, he might have been an idolater. Contemporaneously, he may be an atheist or an agnostic. In either case, he does not recognize the religious validity of the Torah, which to him at best is a human document embodying the culture of the people. He might even grant it historical significance, but would not see in it the divine word which imposes obligations on the people of Israel. Can such sovereignty have halakhic endorsement? Can it be perceived as a fulfillment of the biblical obligation to create a state so that the land might be regarded as the land of Israel in fulfillment of the biblical promise to the patriarch Abraham? The answer, which is at least implicit in the Bible, is affirmative. Many individuals who were practicing idolaters served as monarchs of the ancient kingdoms of Israel and Judah, and the prophetic books of the Bible explicitly refer to them as kings. To the extent that they fulfilled the first obligation of the sovereign, namely, to assure the security of the state and its people, they were apparently entitled to the status of a sovereign.

But further, sovereignty today differs from what it was in ancient days. Then, it consisted of a single person who occupied the throne of a nation. Today, it refers to a variety of functions—executive, legislative, judicial—that are distributed among many individuals. When the powers of government were concentrated in the hands of one person, his religious posture determined the religious character of the government. When several together constitute the sovereign power, the religious quality of the state is not homogeneous. It is normally the resultant of a variety of forces that may well be inconsistent with each other. There are secularists and religiously committed; even among the pious, there are different forms of religious expression such that the practice of some is rejected as unsatisfactory by others. Nevertheless, to the extent that religious individuals and parties exert influence on the government and encourage patterns of legislation that prescribe forms of conduct that are required by the Torah, the contemporary government of Israel has another dimension that can be identified as genuinely religious. In Israel today there are religious courts of justice that adjudicate according to the halakhah in matters of personal status. There is legislation reflecting halakhic requirements of religious conduct, e.g., the obligation in public observance to abide by the laws of the Sabbath and kashrut. And while many of the members of the Knesset supported such legislation for purely political reasons, those who introduced it were inspired primarily by religious considerations. Accordingly, in addition to the fact that the current sovereign power in the Jewish state is committed to the fulfillment of one of the obligations of government, it also responds, though within limitations, to the other obligation of government as well, i.e., it incorporates, at least to some extent, values of Torah in the legislation and organization of the state.

II

The democratic form of government is unobjectionable on halakhic grounds for several reasons, notwithstanding the biblical prescription of monarchy as the preferred form.

First, as has already been noted, the requirement that a government shall be created is implicit in the Almighty's promise to Abraham that his descendants will inherit the land. The type of government that needs to be instituted was not at that point biblically mandated. After the conquest by Joshua, when the tribes lived on the land, the government of the totality of the people appears to have been a loose confederation of relatively independent tribes. It may even have been the case that the tribes utilized modalities of association that reflected democratic principles to guide their interrelationships. For example, the prophetess Deborah complained that the tribe of Reuven refused to join in battle against the Canaanite army led by Sisera and described the tribe in these words, "Among the divisions of Reuven, there were great searchings of the heart,"[11] a procedure very familiar to those accustomed to democracy.

According to those sages who maintained that the monarchial form of government was authorized by the Bible only with hesitation and in anticipation of the demand that the people would ultimately make, it could be argued that a democratic form might even be regarded as preferable by biblical criteria. At least it renders unlikely the accumulation of power and its misuse by a single individual, a state of affairs that occurs frequently in a kingship. A monarch may impose himself on his people as a deity and enforce patterns of conduct biblically prohibited; a democratically elected president is not likely to be transformed in this manner by the intoxication of power.

But further, even according to the sages who insisted that the command to designate a monarch is categorical, that there is an obligation to establish a state governed by an individual who will function as the king, the imperative cannot be fulfilled at the present time. The law requires that such an individual be elevated to sovereignty through the nomination of a prophet and the approval of the Sanhedrin,[12] neither of which institutions currently exists. Rabbi Abraham Isaac Kook argued that under such circumstances, the power to designate a ruler reverts to the people,[13] i.e., democracy is the appropriate form of government.

III

The important question is not whether the Torah allows a democratic form of government but how such a government should be viewed in the context of a *Jewish* state. The problem is that the ideal of a Jewish state and that of a democratic state are often in conflict. For example, if demographic changes were to occur and non-Jews came to outnumber Jews in the Jewish state, the strict application of democratic procedure would enable its citizens, and this would probably happen, to vote the Jewish state out of existence. Such an eventuality could be avoided if a deliberate policy were adopted to give the political goal of a Jewish state priority, and if procedures were instituted to prevent the undesirable outcome from occurring.

Contradictions between two political objectives both of which command allegiance are not unusual in democracies. It has been argued, and correctly, that the twin ideals of a democracy—freedom and equality—are inherently inconsistent. If one pushes the principle of equality to the extreme and insists on its application, for example, in the distribution of material goods, freedom in the marketplace, so essential to a capitalist economy, has to be relinquished. When states encourage competition in the realm of business affairs, they clearly assign to freedom a level of importance greater than that which they grant to equality. Democracies are normally confronted with such dilemmas when they attempt to apply more than one of their ideals in a single context. It is not surprising, therefore, that a similar situation also arises in a democratic Jewish state. Priorities must be determined.

The question is whether, in the democratic state of Israel, its Jewish identity should be assigned greater importance than its democratic character. It may be safely assumed that, among its religious population, such a priority will in fact be maintained. In the religious perspective, the primary reason for the creation of the Jewish state is religious. The goal is to create a political entity that embodies in its structure the precepts and the values of Torah. This is not to say that the religious segment of the population attaches little value to the forms of democracy. On the contrary, this variety of government is treasured almost uniformly throughout the Jewish community. What is intended is that it should be subordinated to a higher purpose, an arrangement which carries the implication that democratic patterns must be so defined that they will not interfere with the achievement of the religious objective.

One might be inclined to argue that the secular and religious segments of the state would agree on the point of priorities. Secular Zionists, after all, involved themselves in the enterprise of creating a Jewish state to solve the "Jewish problem." While antisemitism was not eliminated following the creation of the state of Israel, the state does make available to the Jewish people the power to respond to outbursts of hostility with greater success than heretofore. It seems reasonable that the Jewish people, after enduring intense and endless pain in the course of millennia because of its life in exile, and after a difficult struggle to restore its ancient political condition of freedom and independence, would not allow itself to disappear because of changes in population distribution.

While this claim may still seem eminently reasonable, it is conceivable that the argument may not be altogether convincing for a new generation of secularists who have had no experience with a diaspora bereft of a Jewish state, and for whom the "Jewish problem" may not be, at least to the extent it was heretofore,' a determining factor. Possibly, many in the secularist camp might insist on the greater importance of democracy, even if such a posture might bring with it the possibility of the disappearance of the Jewish state. Whether they would be prepared to adopt this position or not depends on how they assess the value of Jewish identity. The question needs to be asked: Under what conditions would the preservation of the Jewish state inspire greater commitment even among secularists than its democratic character?

Clearly, there are several bases for Jewish commitment. Two have already been mentioned; one derives from religious considerations, and the other has its source in antisemitism. These perhaps are the strongest foundations for the position that the Jewish character of the state must take priority over its democratic arrangements. But to many, neither of these factors is necessarily cogent. Those who take this position may not have adopted a religious perspective and may not be overly concerned about forms of hostility which they never experienced and whose consequences they never directly observed. Some of them may find more meaningful a cultural basis for Jewish commitment. There was, after all, a form of Zionism, in the early days of the movement to create a Jewish state, that sought justification for the enterprise in cultural factors. Others may be more impressed by historical considerations. They might strive for the continuation of a history which in ancient days was quite spectacular and which was abruptly interrupted almost two millennia ago. But one must necessarily wonder whether commitments based on cultural and historical considerations, and even those that are rooted in the "Jewish problem," have sufficient strength to counter the passion for democracy that burns so strongly in so many.

Similar tensions arise because of the adoption of opposing positions with respect to the issue of universalism and particularism. Universalism means that each human being should be equally concerned about the well-being of all mankind and refrain from giving priority to the members of his particular community. It is reflected in the tendency, for example, of a universalistic Jew to be more responsive to the pain of "mankind" than to the agony of the Jews. A particularist would normally adopt the opposite view. He would assign priority to the needs of those who are socially closest to him, without, of course, ignoring those who are beyond the boundaries of his own community.

The tendency to universalism is enforced by a commitment to the democratic principle of equality. This principle applies primarily to the legal and social domains, and is normally translated into an attempt on the part of government to provide for all citizens equality of opportunity with respect to education, possibilities for economic advancement, and social interrelationships. It is also urged in individual conduct. Citizens are encouraged to treat each other in a manner that reflects a commitment to the equality of all men irrespective of their race, religion, or color. The principle of equality in the context of democracy, therefore, means, among other things, a preference for universalism over particularism. One may then subordinate the Jewish identity of the state to democracy because of a prior commitment to democratic ideals or as consequence of an unconditional acceptance of universalism. In any case, the charismatic appeal of both these ideals—democracy and universalism— has historically inspired irresistible passion in many a Jew.

It is precisely this state of affairs that gives rise to serious anxiety about the future of the Jewish state. There is a fundamental difference between Israeli and American democracy. The United States has what is essentially a two-party system. Both parties share a common vision, namely, a society, governed in accordance with democratic procedures, committed to embodying the ideals of freedom and equality in the patterns of American life. They differ in method; one party hopes to accomplish this by utilizing a theory of economics that advocates competition and productivity, and the other seeks to achieve the same end by emphasizing the need to assure every citizen's well-being throughout his life. In Israel, however, the dispute is not about method but vision. One political group seeks to create a Jewish state in which the democratic ideal is paramount; its adherents typically think in secular terms. The other opts for a state which embodies, in maximum form, the ideals of Torah. These groups are adversarial; they do not speak a common language, and on occasion, their differences erupt in violence. This is a most serious potential threat to the well-being of the Jewish state.

A possible response to this state of affairs, at least from the legal standpoint, would be to write a constitution for the state which would incorporate ironclad measures to ensure that its character as a Jewish state will forever be preserved. The task can probably be accomplished in a variety of ways by those well versed in political science. However, while the writing of a constitution would be a most desirable positive measure, it will not solve the problem entirely. Tensions among those who entertain conflicting visions of the Jewish state would remain, and sporadic eruptions might very well occur. The issue is a very serious one, and while it is generally recognized as such, its resolution does not command the attention it deserves. This is one of the very urgent problems facing Israel and is on a par with that of preserving the *security* of the state.

Israel is a Jewish state; it is also a democratic state. Both characteristics need to be preserved, but priorities must be assigned. The Jewish character of the state will not otherwise be ensured. To preserve the state of Israel, certain modalities of democracy must be subordinated to the Jewish ideal.

12

Religion and Social Order: The Moral Component

Since Judaism is a this-worldly religion, it is understandably concerned with the structure of society and the social order. If it were exclusively interested in other-worldly salvation, it would take little note of social affairs. It would then, as is indeed the case with religions that focus on the transcendent alone, concentrate on individuals and the discipline that they must follow to achieve the ultimate spiritual goal, normally interpreted in other-worldly terms. Because Judaism is this-worldly, the character of society is a basic consideration for it.

Further, a moral scheme of some form is an indispensable element in the organization of a society. It is not surprising, therefore, that moral precepts, namely, *mitzvot bein adam laḥavero*, imperatives that prescribe how man shall behave toward his fellow, are central to religious Judaism. The importance of the moral underpinnings of human life is underscored at the beginning of the Book of Genesis. The Bible is primarily concerned with the *destiny* of the Jewish people. The destiny story begins with the twelfth chapter of Genesis, in which God commands Abraham to proceed to the land of Canaan, ultimately to become the land of Israel, where he is to become the progenitor of a great nation that will live in accordance with His will. The initial chapters, however, introduce the moral problem.

The difference between destiny and morality has already been noted. Morality is concerned with rules that guide interpersonal relations. They may be of the negative variety, prohibiting certain forms of conduct, such as theft; they may also require positive patterns of behavior, e.g., helping the sick, giving to the poor. Destiny introduces an ideal or ultimate goal which a people perceives as its historic mission or purpose. The early chapters of Genesis focus on issues that are essentially of the moral variety. The crime of fratricide, a moral transgression, is depicted and condemned in the story of Cain and Abel. The deluge resulted in the eradication of almost all mankind; and Rashi makes the observation that it was primarily due to *hamas*, the violence prevalent among men.[1] The implication is that there are moral imperatives by which the Jew must abide even when he pursues the goals of Jewish destiny.

Even the *akedah*, the binding of Isaac, which is part of the destiny story, was not interpreted by the rabbis as requiring the transcendental suspension of the ethical.[2] That episode was not taken to mean that the Supreme Being would require an arbitrary act of murder merely as a test of a man's faith. On the contrary, it has often been interpreted to signify that the sacrifice of human life simply as a gesture of faith or love of God is *not* an acceptable and legitimate expression of piety. There are occasions which may require the taking of human life in accordance with moral criteria, e.g., by way of punishment for a capital crime or in the case of a justifiable war. But life may not be taken as a mere demonstration of the insignificance of moral precept in the context of religious conduct. Moral behavior, in the Jewish perspective, is a basic *religious* obligation.

I

Judaism recognizes both divine and human components in the foundations of morality; or, to describe the human element with greater accuracy, there is a religious obligation of a moral variety to respond with understanding and compassion to the human condition. This is implicit in the distinction between *din*, the law that expresses the requirement of justice, and *hesed*, the gesture of kindness which is a reflection of the principle of mercy. The demands of justice are formulated in precepts that express God's view of its essence, which is inevitably concealed from human reason and comprehension. The prophet Isaiah declared, "My thoughts are not your thoughts, and your ways are not My ways."[3] Divine kindness is manifested by God's taking human needs and desires into account. "He will fulfill the desires of those who revere Him; He will hear their cries and will help them."[4]

Nor should one suppose that the principles of justice and mercy relate to two different categories of conduct, such that an act to which the principle of justice is applicable is one to which the principle of mercy is irrelevant. To the contrary, the two frequently need to be considered with respect to the same action. Rabbi Joseph B. Soloveitchik, in a public address, once declared that on the tombstone of a celebrated ancestor there appeared the legend *verav ḥesed*, "abundant in mercy." This meant, he explained subsequently in a private conversation, that his grandfather had indeed taken initiatives to alleviate the plight of the poor, the widow, and the orphan. But it meant something more, namely, that in applying the law of the Torah to any case brought to his official attention, he had also taken the principle of *ḥesed* into account.

Din is an expression of justice that is transcendental in essence and is a revelation of the Divine Will. It is the basis for the imposition of obligations which are at times removed from human understanding because they are not necessarily a function of individual or social needs and desires. It is true that precepts of justice are usually regarded as rational because, it is maintained, human beings would have formulated them even had they not been revealed. They would have done so by way of response to the need at all times to guarantee the security of society and to enhance the lives of its citizens— and this indeed is a rational enterprise. Nevertheless, because the rules of justice, *din*, are expressions of God's will, it may be assumed that considerations other than those which in the human perspective are purely rational enter into their formulation. Indeed, there are some rules of *din* that cannot be accounted for in a purely rational way.

There is, for example, the principle of *kovuah*, which means: If an object remains unmoved in its place, the principle of the majority does not apply; if it is moved from its place, it does. By way of illustration—and I select a case which is specifically religious and nonmoral for the sake of ease of exposition—if a cut of meat is found in the public domain in an area where most of the establishments selling this variety of food are kosher, the principle of the majority is applied and the meat is judged to be kosher; if, however, a person buys meat but does not recall where he bought it, even in a place in which kosher establishments outnumber those not kosher, the halakhah perceives such a situation as equivalent to one in which they are equal in number and therefore forbids eating the meat. Now while the distinction between the two cases is clear, the logic, from the human perspective, is hardly compelling.[5]

Or, consider the talmudically delineated difference between *hakhhashah*, contradicting prior witnesses, and *hazamah*, falsifying them. If two witnesses contradict two prior witnesses in regard to some event that is alleged to have taken place, one pair of witnesses claiming that they saw the incident in question, and the other insisting that they were present at the time, observed everything that happened, and that the alleged incident did not take place, then neither set of witnesses is believed. If, however, the second pair testifies, not with respect to the alleged incident but with respect to the first pair of witnesses, declaring, for example, that they could not have witnessed such an incident because they were someplace else when it allegedly occurred, then the second pair is believed but not the first.[6] Again, the distinction is clear, but the logic, from the human standpoint, is not altogether convincing. Indeed, such principles express a divine understanding that is beyond human comprehension.

On the other hand, Judaism recognizes that there are circumstances in which the human condition and not the Divine Will is the factor that should provides the rationale for rules of human conduct. This occurs in situations which require the application of the principle of *hesed*, kindness, or that of *lifnim mishurat hadin*, going beyond the strict requirements of the law, or more dramatically the concept of *tikkun haolam*, the improvement of society. Consider the last of these. It has been noted that the function of the *shofet*, or judge, differs from that of the *melekh*, or king. The former is preoccupied with bringing to man the *inyan elohi*, the divine element, and the focus of the latter is *tikkun haolam*, the improvement of society. The king must consider human needs, such as security, quality of life, etc. He must enact legislation that will assure the safety, well-being, and preservation of the community. The laws utilized by the *shofet* are explicit in the Written and Oral Law. The laws applied by the sovereign are the invention, as need arises, of those who have the power to enact them. They respond to the human condition.[7]

These two principles—*din* and *ḥesed*, the application of divine principles of justice and responding to the human factor—are also essential in interpersonal relations. We may relate to others in the spirit of justice, always insisting on principle; or we may focus on the need to alleviate the suffering endemic to the human species, or we may do both.[8]

II

How are we to accommodate two principles which appear to require contradictory courses of action. The demands of justice, reflecting the perspective of the Divine Mind, are often inconsistent with those of mercy, which prompt responses manifested in gestures of compassion. The example that immediately comes to mind is that of the criminal who is seeking mercy in the courtroom. To exonerate is to defy the demand of justice that a penalty appropriate to the crime be administered. How then can the moral conflict between the divine and the human be resolved?

It has been argued that *din*, justice, and *ḥesed* and *lifnim mishurat hadin*, both expressions of mercy, are included under the generic concept of halakhah, the Torah way of life.[9] This means that while justice is an essential norm in God's relation to man, the Almighty Himself seeks to apply the principle of *ḥesed* and to be responsive to human frailties and concerns. In point of fact He is even more responsive, for He, more than any terrestrial being, is aware of human weaknesses and incapacities. The contradiction is accordingly incorporated into the halakhic scheme of things. How then does the halakhah deal with this obvious inconsistency?

The rabbinic interpreters of the Bible provide an immediate and crucial response. It is, in the last analysis, a matter of priorities! There is a well-known comment by Rashi at the beginning of Genesis to the effect that God originally wanted to create a world that would be guided exclusively in accordance to the principle of justice; when, however, He determined that under such circumstances, mankind could not survive, he attached to justice the principle of mercy and assigned it priority.[10] The essential point of this comment is not that mercy was introduced as a companion principle to assure the continued existence of mankind, but that mankind's permanence requires that mercy be assigned a status prior to and more important than justice.

The tension that the contradiction between justice and mercy generates derives simply from the recognition that both principles make legitimate but incompatible claims which cannot be accommodated. Tension of this type is not infrequent in human experience. It often happens that twin ideals or goals are projected in such a way that the requirements of both cannot be satisfied simultaneously. This is the case, for example, with the ideals of Torah and *madda*. When we are engaged in the personally satisfying enterprise of human creativity, which is the preoccupation of those involved with *madda*, we are not able to focus on our relationship to the Divine Being, which is the goal of Torah. This variety of tension is also characteristic of *din* and *ḥesed*, justice and mercy. In all such instances, inconsistencies are resolved by assigning priorities and defining them with relative precision in rules of conduct.

The application of both principles is not a requirement in all circumstances. A hardened and unrepentant criminal who has been condemned to suffer a severe sentence is not normally perceived as entitled to compassion. The Bible declares, for example, that in the case of one who has seduced another to idolatry, "Do not close your eyes to what he is doing, do not have pity on him and do not cover up for him."[11] But this is the exception rather than the rule. Even in the instance of one who is alleged to have committed murder, the Torah commands the members of the Sanhedrin trying the case to exert themselves to exonerate the accused. This is required, according to talmudic interpretation, by the biblical imperative, "The assembly shall judge, and the assembly shall save,"[12] i.e., it must be the purpose of the court to bend every effort, in terms of the identification of the facts and the interpretation of the law, to save the accused. Judicial practices that the sages put in place, basing themselves on this verse, had as a consequence that even many who were guilty escaped capital punishment. This was a dramatic expression of the priority of mercy over justice. But there are others.

The innocent are always entitled to mercy. There are, after all, circumstances in which the principle of justice is not of crucial import. At times, the individual seeking an act of compassion is not a criminal; he is merely in serious trouble. One could argue, as does the rugged individualist, that justice requires that one give to another only that which represents an obligation—arising out of a liability due perhaps to an act of borrowing or to a loss or injury inflicted upon the other. At this point halakhah intervenes and declares that this is a circumstance par excellence where an act of *ḥesed* is mandatory.

The halakhah requires mercy even on occasions of transgression if the latter is accompanied by an act of penitence. The Talmud records a series of categories of sin for which an individual can atone and achieve forgiveness, but each requires as a prerequisite an act of penitence. The sages note that the sound of the shofar on Rosh Hashanah reminds the Jew to modify his actions, i.e., to perform gestures of penitence, and if he does, the Almighty withdraws from the seat of justice and places Himself on the seat of mercy,[13] that is to say, He rearranges His priorities with respect to the petitioning individual. Maimonides puts it as follows: "Even though penitence and prayer are always desirable, they are particularly desirable and *accepted immediately* during the ten days of penitence between Rosh Hashanah and Yom Kippur, as it is written, `Seek God when He can be found.'"[14] If an individual guilty of a serious transgression performs an act of contrition then, in many instances, especially where the offense is not subject to sentencing by a human court, he is immediately and fully forgiven. The requirements of justice are completely subordinated to those of mercy. This does not mean that an act of contrition is, by itself and at all times, sufficient to effect full pardon; there are occasions when, according to rabbinic instruction, pain and suffering are also prerequisite.[15] Such pain is almost inevitable when the transgression or crime is subject to punishment by a human court, in which case the prescribed sentence must be administered. Nevertheless, the act of forgiveness which is inherently a merciful act is, on the rabbinic view, essential even when punishment is in order. The man who stole must return to its owner the object that he appropriated even while he must seek pardon from both his victim and the Almighty. The man who committed murder and was found guilty must suffer the penalty even while he is required to confess and ask forgiveness before he surrenders his life. The element of mercy consists in his being restored to grace. If, however, the requirements of mercy were completely subordinated to those of justice, the act of penitence, however sincere, would not justify the act of forgiveness under any circumstances and in whatever form.

There is also a form of mercy that is based on consanguinity. Relatives, if they are sufficiently close, are not permitted to testify in the courtroom either for or against each other. Friends who are attached to each other by strong bonds of affection may, however, do so.[16] The reason for this is not that the sentiment of love prevents the adoption by witnesses of the posture of objectivity that is essential for the application of rules of justice—otherwise friends would not have been permitted to testify—but that blood relations are obligated to behave toward each other in accordance with the principle of mercy at all times, without getting involved in processes that reflect the application of rules of justice.

There are occasions when justice and mercy need to be perceived as complementary, i.e., when the failure to apply both leads to injustice. In such a case, mercy is not merely prior to justice; it is one of its indispensable components. The classic example is that of stealing a loaf of bread. The crime is far less heinous if it is perpetrated by one whose children are starving than by one whose fortunes are not spectacular but who could manage to provide for his family reasonably well without resorting to theft. In order to assess a situation adequately to determine what justice requires, attention must be paid to the facts to which the principles of law are to be applied. But this is not always taken into account. Some demand justice in abstraction from the detailed circumstances in which a law was violated, in which case a deprived individual and one who is prosperous, each of whom purloined food, are regarded as equally guilty of theft. The principle of mercy, however, requires an assessment of the entire context in which the criminal act occurred in order to find, in the conditions of poverty, extenuating circumstances sufficient to justify leniency to the impoverished individual. Justice must be mediated by truth to achieve its own aims; and when truth intervenes, the human condition is necessarily taken into account, that is to say, mercy is applied as well.

Of course, not all varieties of mercy are dependent on objectivity for their application. Sympathy may prompt a gesture of compassion toward one who is undeserving. A person visibly in pain will inspire offers of assistance without any awareness on the part of the willing donor of the context in which assistance is requested, i.e., the character of the recipient and whether he is indeed entitled by some moral criterion to generosity. Certainly the love of a parent for a child will stimulate dramatic acts of generosity even if the parent knows that his offspring is not deserving. These are gestures of mercy independent of objective considerations. In such instances, the context in which the gesture of mercy is petitioned is not at all taken into account. But there is, of course, a form of mercy which depends on objectivity. It is one that perceives all features of the criminal context as potentially relevant, and it claims that principles of justice are not to be implemented in the abstract because to do so is very often to translate a just *law* into an *act* of rank injustice.

The resolution of the contradiction between justice and mercy by affirming priorities, therefore, does not amount to the elimination of either. It merely provides a means of dealing constructively with the tension that it generates. To affirm priority is not to insist on exclusivity; it is not to practice compassion under all circumstances. It is merely to suggest how to live with contradiction. When we act on a priority, we are confident that we are doing that which is right even while we may continue to experience the tension that arises out of the contradiction.

III

Even while the resolution of contradictions by assigning priorities may be perceived as relatively innocuous when the individual is exclusively taken into account, it generates much more concern when the social consequences of his conduct are also taken into consideration. Notwithstanding, assigning priority to mercy is relevant in the expanded social context as well.

Justice and its expressions in law are indispensable conditions of social order. The unexceptional application of mercy and compassion in all instances to which they are relevant could lead to anarchy. If the one who commits a crime always anticipates escaping the consequences, there is nothing to prevent him from continuing with his antisocial behavior and inflicting endless hardships on the community. Even if the criminal is treated with compassion in most instances, the rule of law is weakened and society suffers from an increase in anarchy, with all of its potentially devastating results. As the talmudic sages put it, "He who is compassionate to the cruel is eventually cruel to the compassionate,"[17] that is to say, the suffering of the innocent is an unavoidable consequence of the display of mercy to the cruel. On the other hand, without the quality of compassion, humanity could not survive. This is the thrust of the rabbinic commentary cited above, which affirms the priority of mercy over justice. If everyone always and uncompromisingly demanded from his counterpart all that he perceives to be his due, antagonism and confrontation would be constant and uninterrupted, and social life would be hopelessly mired in conflict. When mercy was assigned supremacy over justice, therefore, it was intended to apply to the social arena as well, that is to say, such a priority was perceived to be to the advantage of society as a whole. Compassion must remain a predominant consideration in the formulation of social and judicial policy. But it should be understood that priority was not granted unconditionally. In the context of the judicial disposition of criminals, for example, mercy could indeed be appropriate if the defendant is genuinely contrite and penitential, so that there is some justifiable expectation of modified behavior, but not otherwise.

IV

The talmudic assignment of the laws of justice to a secondary status is perhaps most evident in the following passage:

> R. Judah b. Korha says: Settlement by arbitration is a meritorious act, for it is written, "Execute the judgment of truth and peace in your gates."[18] Surely where there is strict justice, there is no peace, and where there is peace, there is no strict justice! But what is the kind of justice with which peace abides? We must say: Arbitration.[19]

Arbitration is the result of the introduction of an element of generosity, i.e., mercy, into the process. To accept arbitration is to allow a third person to decide a case without taking the strict requirements of justice into account. It is an arrangement wherein each of the litigants exhibits readiness to surrender that which justly belongs to him in order to resolve the matter. The dispute is not terminated by the application of the law but by the spirit of generosity. Jewish law recognizes the priority of arbitration to adjudication because it is committed to the ideal of social tranquility.[20] The insistence on the rigorous application of justice promotes conflict and hostility even after a decision has been rendered by the court. It is preferable to resolve a dispute in an amicable way even if justice is not fully served.[21]

We find ourselves, accordingly, confronting a striking paradox. A religion whose emphasis is on law, the quintessential expression of justice, acknowledges that the full attainment of its goal, given human nature, is impossible, and consequently advocates the primacy of mercy in order to assure the uninterrupted continuity of mankind. This reinforces a view classic in Jewish life to the effect that the purpose of the law is primarily to serve as a pedagogic instrument for shaping and molding a religious and moral character among those whom it obligates. The principal purpose of the law is not the punishment of transgressors—just though this enterprise may be.

13

Religion and the Social Order: The Element of Destiny

A social order may reflect elements of destiny as well as moral modalities. In the case of a democratic state which requires a social structure based essentially on principles of justice, freedom, and equality, i.e., the requirements of social morality, issues of destiny are raised by its diverse cultural groups independently of political considerations. Different religions may entertain conceptions of destiny that are defined in other-worldly terms, and secular communities may characterize them in terms of the achievement of ideal social arrangements for mankind. In the Jewish perception of the social structure of a Jewish state which is both democratic and Jewish, the ideals and aims associated with Jewish destiny also contribute unique elements to Jewish political life. This is especially the case if the Jewish character of the state is given priority over its democratic status. It should be noted in this connection that even secular Jews, who regard democracy as of greater consequence to the Jewish state than its Jewish quality, frequently interpret the meaning of their Jewish identity in terms of destiny, though they are not always able to give a satisfactory account of its contents. In their view too, therefore, to the extent that the democratic state is Jewish, the element of destiny is relevant to the political life of the Jewish state. Our concern here, however, will be the element of destiny religiously defined and its implications for the order and arrangement of the Jewish society and the Jewish state.

Jewish destiny consists of two parts: (a) the historical process, i.e., the events that constitute the story of the Jew in a gentile world, and (b) the historical goal, i.e., the messianic aspirations of the Jewish people. The first deals with the factual character of the Jewish historical experience, and among other things, how the status of the Jew in the non-Jewish world was reflected in patterns of Jewish living. This historical process is not accidental or arbitrary, at least not entirely so. An example of a principle which is taken to be exemplified in Jewish history is implicit in the divine declaration received by the matriarch Rebecca: "And the Eternal said unto her: Two nations are in thy womb, and two peoples will emerge from you. One people will be stronger than the other, and the elder shall serve the younger."[1]

This pronouncement does not refer to a goal which the descendants of Isaac and Rebecca are destined to achieve. It is, rather, a description of certain characteristics of the process which will unfold in the history of the Jewish people. The second, which consists of a vision that portrays the historic goal of the Jewish people is expressed, for example, in the following celebrated passage:

> And many people shall go and say: Come let us go up to the mountain of the Lord, to the house of the God of Jacob; and He will teach us His ways, and we will walk in His path; for out of Zion shall go forth the law and the word of the Lord from Jerusalem.[2]

Jewish destiny, accordingly, involves both process and goal; it is reflected in many of the historical events as they in fact occur and unfold, and it projects a conception of the ultimate to be achieved in the end of days. It has something to say about the world here and now as well as the world to come.

I

The Bible and the rabbinic sages were very much preoccupied with the process of Jewish history. Several biblical passages focus on it. At the Covenant Among the Parts, Abraham is informed that his descendants will find themselves in a land which is not theirs (Egypt), where they will be enslaved, and from which they will ultimately be redeemed.[3] Reference has already been made to the declaration received by the matriarch Rebecca concerning the inevitable and unceasing struggle between the descendants of Jacob and of Esau. It was also a biblical prophecy that the people of Israel, settled in its own land, would transgress against the law of God, suffer exile from its patrimony, and ultimately repent and return.[4]

The rabbis elaborated upon these biblical characterizations of the historical process. Rashi, for example, writes, "It is a law, well known, that Esau hates Jacob."[5] This metaphorical statement enunciates the claim that the descendants of Jacob are unceasingly subject to the affliction of antisemitism, a phenomenon that has had ample confirmation in Jewish history. Nachmanides sees in the biographies of the patriarchs indications of the history of their progeny. It is his judgment, reflecting a commentary in the Midrash, that "all that happened to the fathers is a sign of that which will happen to the children."[6] Indeed the story of the patriarchs is the microcosm that reflects the macrocosm of Jewish history. There is also a talmudic passage:

> Caesarea and Jerusalem! If you are told that both are destroyed, do not believe it; that both are thriving, do not believe it; that Caesarea is destroyed and Jerusalem is thriving or that Jerusalem is destroyed and Caesarea is thriving, this you may believe.[7]

In this commentary, Caesarea and Jerusalem are symbolic of two antithetic and antagonistic cultures—Jerusalem, of course, symbolizes that of the people of Israel—that are constantly at odds. It amounts to the claim that the struggle between them is continuous and that both cannot prosper simultaneously.

II

We may begin with some general observations. First, the claim that the process of Jewish history is, at least to some extent, controlled by certain principles relating Jewish historical experience to that of other nations implies that Jewish history is not irrelevant to world history. The principles of the historical process described herein suggest an ongoing struggle in which Jews are at times defeated but in other instances victorious. This is part of the drama of redemption. Even defeat could be regarded as essential to the redemptive process. For example, the wandering of the people of Israel for forty years in the desert, which could be interpreted as a defeat at the hands of the

Divine Being, was not so much a punishment as it was an attempt to transform the character of the Jew so that he could move forward in the pursuit of his historic destiny. One could argue that there are occasions and even lengthy periods in Jewish history which are indeed inconsequential to universal history in that they constitute periods of *hester panim*, the "hiding of [God's] Face." During such epochs, the people of Israel suffers and its experiences, devastating as they are, can hardly be regarded as relevant to the redemptive process. Indeed, enduring afflictions that possess no redeeming value, the Holocaust for example, may be essential to the meaning of *hester panim*. But there are also large spans of Jewish history which bear directly on world history. The Jewish historical process will end with the realization of the historic goal, namely, the messianic era, which marks the conclusion of the histories of all peoples.

Further, this process need not have as an inevitable consequence, and as its last step, the achievement of the historic goal. It may, but it need not. There is a rabbinic commentary on a phrase in Isaiah which refers to the ultimate redemption and declares, *be'itah ahishenah*, "I will hasten it in its time."[8] The rabbis note a contradiction: if it is hastened, it is not in its time, and if it arrives on time, it is not hastened. They reply, "If they deserve it, it will be hastened; if they do not deserve it, it will arrive on time."[9] Evidently, the Jewish historical process will reflect guiding principles of Jewish history even while it may not flow inevitably into the realization of the ultimate historic vision.

III

A more detailed consideration needs to be given to some of the particular "laws" of historical process as formulated in the Bible and the rabbinic commentaries. One of these, cited above, is the unrelieved conflict between the two cultures represented by Caesarea and Jerusalem. The emphasis in this commentary is not on an antagonism between the *peoples* symbolized by Caesarea and Jerusalem, but on the inherent contradiction between the *cultures* represented by these two celebrated ancient cities. The incommensurability of these cultures is expressed in several ways. First, the Greek and Roman cultures were idolatrous, endorsing the worship of immanent objects and forces, while Judaism is spiritually monotheistic, advocating the worship of one transcendental Being. Second, the primary focus of Greece and Rome was on the true, as revealed in philosophical study, and the beautiful, as manifested in such aesthetic activities as sculpture and drama, while Judaism is fundamentally interested in the holy, i.e., the service of God. Finally, there is a basic opposition even with regard to the notion of "the good." The Greeks and Romans interpreted the good in eudaemonistic terms, i.e., the good is that in human experience which contributes to human happiness. In Judaism, the good is defined transcendentally, namely, obedience to the will of God. It is the last point that is particularly important for understanding the antagonism between the two cultures here described. To find the clues for human happiness in the facts of human nature and social conditions leads to conclusions substantially at odds with those arrived at from the premise that the ultimate good is a life fully in accord with the will of the Supreme Being.

The opposition of Greece and Rome to Israel is manifested in still another way. There is a struggle for supremacy between the nations symbolized by Esau and the people of Israel. This is the essential point of the declaration to the biblical Rebecca cited above, "One people will be stronger than the other, and the elder shall serve the younger." Here the emphasis is not on *cultures* but on *peoples* or *nations*.

Clearly, the people of Israel defines itself not merely in terms of culture; it was, after all, a people before it accepted the Sinaitic obligations. It became such in Egypt, and even while suffering the afflictions of slavery, it perceived its identity, not essentially in being the target of persecution, but rather in being descended from the patriarchs Abraham, Isaac, and Jacob. This family distinction prevails even today and may be even more significant than the cultural.

Adherence to a culture is more readily relinquished than family ties. It is obviously the case that a very large segment of the Jewish community today identifies itself as Jewish even while it substantially repudiates commitments of a Jewish nature. It is significant that Jewish identity is halakhically interpreted as primarily a function of circumstances of birth. An impressive indication of the depth of family feeling that prevails between Jew and Jew is the fact that a Jew in New York is seriously concerned about his counterpart in India or China when the latter finds himself in grave difficulties, though he has never seen him and has no relationship whatsoever with him. Being a Jew is a primarily a family affair.[10]

It can be argued, and I believe with a degree of cogency, that in significant measure, the opposition to the Jew and even hatred for him on the part of the non-Jew is a response to patterns of conduct that are consequences of this sense of family distinctiveness. The Jew's tendency to relate to his community as he does to his family leads to behavior that differentiates him from those beyond the boundaries of Jewish life. This occurs, for example, in his resolve to live in isolation from the gentile world and in the company of his compatriots. It is a historical fact that the Jew was not forced into the ghetto; he adopted it voluntarily. Doing so made it easier for him to live completely as a Jew, but in addition, it increased his sense of comfort and security when he knew that he was surrounded by family on whom he could depend for support and protection. The Jew's tendency to remain separate and apart was often interpreted by gentiles as a rejection of the non-Jew.

The philanthropic inclination of the Jew, as it is expressed in relation to the Jewish community, is legendary. It is not exhibited to the same extent toward those beyond the boundaries of Jewish life. This is not due to an absence of concern for the non-Jew; it is a demonstration of a stronger and deeper commitment for other Jews, who are perceived as members of the same family. The non-Jew does not always appreciate this motivation; indeed he may see it, too, as a rejection of non-Jews, with the not infrequent result that resentment is ignited.

There are dramatic contemporary illustrations of the power wielded by this sense of family. The state of Israel was facing an economic crisis of major proportions. An opportunity arose to receive one million Jewish immigrants from the Soviet Union. Doing so would represent an increase of about twenty percent in its population with the potentially disastrous effect that its economic problems would be exacerbated. The Jewish state did not flinch from the challenge and immediately extended an enthusiastic hand of welcome. A nation that is guided exclusively by normal national modalities, i.e., by considerations of self-interest, would not have adopted this course of action. It would have tried to protect its citizens from conditions that would aggravate their economic problems. But Israel was prompted by other, nonpolitical considerations, namely, a feeling of family solidarity and a concomitant sense of destiny.

The Law of Return itself must be perceived as a riddle by the nations of the world. It declares that any Jew is entitled to immediate admission and citizenship in the state of Israel. Further, this prerogative is in effect irrespective of ideological or political commitments. Such political behavior, which is in effect exclusionary, in that it denies to non-Jews prerogatives granted to Jews, and is rooted in modalities of conduct that are appropriate to a family rather than a nation, constitutes a distinctiveness that separates the Jew and isolates him from those outside the boundaries of the Jewish community.

To the extent that the Jewish community defines itself as a family, it becomes vulnerable to the charge of racism. Indeed, the emphasis upon birth can be interpreted as the desire to preserve racial purity, a reading that is obviously false in relation to the Jewish people in view of its willingness to admit converts. It can also be interpreted, and correctly, in terms of the resolve to preserve the character of a family even when the community becomes a state, but this approach strikes the rest of the world as strange and paradoxical. It is easier and, for those who seek to objectify their impulse to hate, more gratifying to adopt the abhorrent racial interpretation. The Jewish persistence in applying to the community parameters normally characteristic of a family led to the repugnant and abominable "Zionism is racism" resolution embraced unabashedly by the United Nations.

This leads to a second "law" describing the relationship of Jews to the nations. "It is a law, well known, that Esau hates Jacob." The people who are symbolized by Esau are not merely confrontational and adversarial; they are in fact hostile. Now, opposition need not necessarily be translated into hatred. In a democratic society, members of opposing political parties are often friends; they socialize with each other and are often married to each other. In the relation of Jew and gentile, opposition frequently turns to antipathy.

It has been argued that the hostility toward the Jew directed at him by the gentile world is due primarily to the fact that he regards himself as "chosen." It is said that this is an arrogant posture which people resent. The judgment is, in all likelihood, erroneous. In a sense, all religious groups regard themselves as chosen, though they opt to express their chosenness in different ways. When the Christian community spread death and destruction among the members of the Jewish community with reckless abandon during the period of the Crusades and the era of the Inquisition, its adherents displayed a form of contempt for Jews that was in effect an assertion of superiority far more intolerable than is the mere verbal assertion of chosenness. When the followers of Islam seek to establish the supremacy of their creed by the sword, they make a powerful claim to being chosen. It is not the chosenness of the Jew but the social and political ramifications of a distinctiveness, both religious and sociological, that is perceived as strange and alien that are ultimately the root of malice.

When nations engage in battle, each seeks victory; when the relation is one of hostility, the goal of the aggressive party is often persecution and even annihilation. This is the basis for the slings and arrows of outrageous antisemitism directed at the Jewish people across the centuries. It is precisely because hatred is added to opposition in the relation of Jew and gentile that the Jewish people often feels isolated and beleaguered. Among the nations of the world, and the Jewish people is an outstanding exception, confrontation derives from the imperialist impulse and a desire for victory. A modern political thinker traced the roots of war to three factors; he wrote, "In the nature of man, we find three principal causes of quarrel. First, competition; second, diffidence; thirdly, glory"[11]—but hatred was not perceived to be among them. Hatred is, however, a fundamental consideration in the struggle of the people of Israel with the non-Jewish world.

This is not to say that hatred is entirely absent from confrontations among non-Jewish nations. It is present, but in most instances in a derivative rather than primary form. If someone interferes in another's pursuit of self-interest, he may very well arouse antipathy which is often dissipated when the obstacle to the other's well-being is lifted. It is well known that nations at war will join forces overnight if suddenly threatened by a third and more powerful nation. Here hatred is a function of being perceived as frustrating another's national interest. When, however, hatred is fundamental and unconditional, it occurs irrespective of considerations of self-interest. It is manifested, for example, in the pursuit of programs which actualize hostility even while they are inimical to the nation that initiated them.[12] The Nazis remained determined to implement their brutal agenda of extermination even when it was interfering seriously with their war effort. There is a variety of war that is based, not on competition, glory, or fear, but on naked hostility.

This is the ground for the Jewish tendency to defensiveness. Jews today do not suffer from a persecution complex, i.e., a groundless fear that is an exaggerated response to a single attempt to exterminate them, viz., the Holocaust—as if that devastating experience were not in itself sufficient to justify the defensive posture. It arises rather from the Jew's perception that he is, and historically has been, vulnerable, not merely to opposition, but to hatred. It convinces him that even in the best of circumstances antisemitism is very much a part of the landscape of Jewish life. Because of the unique character of the Jewish people and the antagonism that it arouses, it must necessarily possess an instrument powerful enough to defend and protect itself against the assaults mounted regularly upon it by its enemies, i.e., a Jewish state. Indeed, many once maintained that such a political arrangement would normalize the condition of the Jew; that is to say, that hatred for the Jew would disappear. Instead, the reverse was accomplished; the creation of the state merely added still another target and on a larger, macrocosmic scale for the hostility of the antisemite. A dramatic demonstration of the inherent difficulty involved in any attempt to eliminate hostility for the Jew, and reference has already been made to this, was the enactment by the United Nations of the hideous "Zionism is racism" resolution even while the state of Israel was in existence, a resolution which remained the official doctrine of that august body for a decade.

IV

Another "law" which according to biblical doctrine enters as a crucial factor into the Jewish historical process is of a moral character, that is to say, it does not perceive historical events as natural effects of physical causes but as consequences of obedience or transgression. The result of disobeying the divine commandments is punishment, a state of affairs described in considerable detail in the Bible.[13] A form of punishment particularly severe is expulsion from the land, an eventuality that materialized twice in Jewish history. The prayer book contains the judgment oft repeated, "Because of our sins were we exiled from the land."[14] While this law is frequently adumbrated, the manner of its precise operation is not clearly defined, i.e., it is not always certain when the course of actual events instantiates it. A few modalities of its application, however, can be offered.

First, the experience of pain is not always an indication of punishment. Pain frequently has a constructive use: (a) to mold character—"You shall know in your heart that as a father chastises his son, the Lord your God chastises you";[15] (b) to cultivate a moral perspective with respect to values—"He caused you pain, He made you hungry . . . to let you know that man does not live by bread alone."[16] The rabbis of the Talmud fully adopt this view and accordingly speak of "pain inflicted because of love,"[17] basing this assessment on the verse, "God chastises him whom He loves."[18] The sages struggle with the problem as to when pain is so severe that it can only be perceived as related to punishment, but they do not arrive at a definitive answer.

Further, one cannot read human and Jewish history as an exemplification, without exception, of moral laws. The sages recognize the many instances in which "righteous suffer and scoundrels prosper."[19] Rashi comments, by way of explaining the concept of "pain inflicted because of love," "The Almighty chastises them in this world in order to enhance their reward in the world to come."[20] This implies that while the thesis that justice is invariably exemplified in human affairs is valid as a matter of faith, it is useless to attempt to demonstrate it on the basis of empirical evidence.

The same position is implied by another rabbinic commentary to the effect that there are circumstances when the righteous suffer, and grievously, though they are not themselves guilty. Thus, Rashi writes, on the verse which declares that mankind will be destroyed in a deluge, "In every era characterized by unchastity and violence, a cataclysm strikes the world and destroys the good with the bad."[21] This is an explicit rabbinic recognition that the principle of justice is not invariably exemplified in a terrestrial context.

The idea of *hester panim*, the hiding of the Face, incorporates the same idea. The notion of the Supreme Being withdrawing from the world presupposes, among other things, that the moral law will be suspended, i.e., that the pious will suffer together with the scoundrel.

It follows that while the belief in the universal application of justice is indispensable to the religious posture, it can only be assumed if the world to come is included in the span of time in which this law is exemplified, but it will not find unexceptional application in the world here and now.

V

The second component in the idea of Jewish destiny is the historic goal the Jewish people and mankind are ultimately to achieve. In effect it refers to the final redemption that will be the heritage of all humanity in the messianic era. The Jewish idea of redemption includes several components: (a) the redemption is this-worldly rather than other-worldly; (b) a Jewish state and a Holy Temple in

Jerusalem are indispensable prerequisites to redemption; (c) the ultimate human condition will be one in which mankind is united in the service of God.[22] These notions have penetrated the Jewish psyche and instilled attitudes that have had crucial social and political ramifications.[23]

(a) The belief in a terrestrial rather than celestial concept of redemption is at the basis of Jewish optimism with respect to the outcome of the historical process. Other faiths affirm the legitimacy of hope, but in general they have in mind hope for a better life in another, transcendent, purely spiritual realm. The Jewish religion supports the expectation that the social and political processes occurring in the world here and now will ultimately be translated into an arrangement in which justice and peace will be the universal and unexceptional share of all mankind. This expectation of fulfillment in the historical realm is indeed a distinguishing characteristic of Jewish life.

Jewish optimism is translated into a tenacious determination to assure self-preservation—both as a people and as a way of life. Other ancient cultures and peoples may have disappeared from the face of the earth, but the people of Israel believes that it is destined to survive. The anguish and tribulations it has experienced across the centuries might have prompted it as a group to withdraw from the earth's stage, to surrender to those who on so many occasions have sought its extermination, were it not for the irrepressible optimistic conviction that in the end there will be national resurrection and religious restoration.

It should be noted that this optimism is not identical to the belief, entertained by mankind in the era of the Enlightenment, in inevitable progress. That belief was nourished by the scientific revolution and the emancipation of mankind through the introduction of political democracy. It was not a belief that withstood the test of time. Technology born of science threatens to destroy mankind, and democracy does not ensure that individuals, in pursuing their own interests, will inevitably act in a manner that is best for humanity. The Jewish approach entertains the belief in the *possibility* of progress; this belief is supported by the conviction that mankind has the capacity to act in consonance with moral precepts which, in turn, would have the effect of creating a just and peaceful society. It is also convinced that the ultimate redemption is inevitable because, in any case, it will arrive through divine intervention, irrespective of humanity's moral condition.

It should be noted once more that the variety of optimism that characterizes Jewish life is not based on an assessment of the consequences of actual states of affairs. There is a form of optimism—its rational variety—that is rooted in the perception that the relevant facts justify the expectation that one's desires will materialize. The optimism intrinsic to Judaism emerges out of faith and is often experienced in defiance of the facts. It is, in effect, an expression of the belief that the facts can be transformed no matter how oppressive and overwhelming they might be.

These two varieties of optimism have diverging political consequences. The optimism that results from an objective assessment of facts tends to support and strengthen existing political arrangements. An American general once said, "To win, you have to get there first with the most." If an army satisfies these conditions, optimism is rationally justified, with the result that the political arrangements of the country represented on the battlefield by the army in question will in all likelihood be secured. The optimism that is independent of facts tends to work in a political direction opposite to that which obtains, because the prevailing arrangement is usually inconsistent with the faith on which the optimistic attitude is based. For example, notwithstanding the improbability, from a rational perspective, that a Jewish state could be recreated millennia after its destruction, optimism nourished the movement that led to its reestablishment.

(b) The idea of the messianic era also includes, as an ingredient, a return to the ancient homeland and the rebuilding of the Holy Temple. Faith in that goal inspired within the Jewish community a form of religious Zionism which sought the recreation of a Jewish state. It was an indispensable prerequisite to ultimate redemption.

It should be noted that even in the secular community Zionism was a political movement with messianic roots. Though secularists discarded their religious commitments, they could not dissociate themselves from attitudes and ideas sunk so deep in the Jewish psyche that they were, in effect, part of the intellectual climate of Jewish life. These ideas had been unconsciously absorbed and prompted Jewish attitudes without revealing their source. Messianic aspirations were paramount among them. It is for this reason that secular Jews were in the forefront of all those social and political movements that offered the promise of redemption for mankind, e.g., socialism, communism, civil rights. They had messianic overtones. The resolve of secular Zionists to solve the Jewish problem was redemptive in nature.

Jewish history is, accordingly, intimately related to world history not only insofar as the historical process is concerned, i.e., the inevitable and frequent confrontations between the descendants of Jacob and of Esau, but also with respect to the ultimate end of that process. The redemption of mankind presupposes the ingathering of Jewish exiles, the restoration of the Jewish homeland, and the rebuilding of the Holy Temple. For the religious Jew, in pursuing these objectives, he is simultaneously striving for a state of blessedness for all mankind.

(c) The ultimate redemption is religious in character. It requires that mankind be united in the service of God. As the liturgy of the High Holy Days puts it, we pray that all humanity "will form one association to do Thy will with perfect hearts."[24] Many attempts have been made in the course of history to achieve a utopia, i.e., a redemptive state of affairs which consists of a rearrangement of social relations by human effort, and without the intervention of a Supreme Being, in such a way that universal justice and peace will be assured. These have uniformly been unsuccessful. The ultimate redemption is to be messianic in nature, i.e., the perfect society requires, as a precondition to its existence, that mankind shall unite in the service of God. Therein lies the promise and the hope of universal well-being.

14

Halakhah and Relevance

The question is sometimes asked whether halakhic Judaism is relevant. To put the question this way, however, is in effect to prejudge the issue. It is, at least implicitly, to declare that the demand for relevance is legitimate, that halakhic Judaism, therefore, should be relevant, and that the crucial question is whether it does indeed meet this requirement. In fact such an assumption may be unwarranted. The important question is not whether halakhic Judaism is relevant but whether it should attempt to be relevant. Is being relevant important?

This question can be satisfactorily resolved only if it is noted that the term "relevance" is notoriously ambiguous. There is at least one sense of the term in which halakhic Judaism should not strive to be relevant. The definition in question is the following: something A is relevant to some other thing B if A conforms to the requirements of B. According to this definition, the insistence that halakhic Judaism (A) be relevant means that it should satisfy the requirements of contemporary human experience (B). The objection to this demand for relevance is that it turns contemporary human experience into the standard and imposes on Judaism the requirement that it undergo a metamorphosis in order to align itself with that standard. When this occurs, Judaism is inevitably transformed. New denominations of Judaism, at odds with the traditional point of view, arise in Jewish life.

The demand for relevance has at times been contrasted with the claim of authenticity. The latter requires that existing patterns of Jewish life be consistent with the classic sources of the Jewish religion. The insistence on relevance implies that contemporary experience is the criteria by which Jewish life today is to be judged, while the preference for authenticity assigns that status to Torah prescriptions. These two goals require intellectual gestures that are polar opposites. If the demand for relevance necessitates a transformation of Judaism to render it consistent with what are essentially alien models, then it is incompatible with the need to live Judaism authentically. At least in the halakhic perspective, the choice is clear: authenticity is the only acceptable option.

There is another meaning of "relevance" which renders trivial the question whether Judaism is relevant, namely, A is relevant to B if the elements of A are applicable to B. In the case under discussion, A consists of the laws of Torah, and B, the facts of human experience. On this interpretation, there is no problem at all with respect to the relevance of Judaism. The laws of the Sabbath, the festivals, kashrut, etc., are indeed applicable to specific realms of experience—the Sabbath to the seventh day of the week, kashrut to the variety of foods available for human consumption, etc. The question whether Judaism is relevant could not possibly have been based on this meaning of the term.

I

There are two other meanings of "relevance," however, both of which justify the demand that Judaism be relevant. The first defines "relevance" in terms of logical consistency, i.e., A is relevant to B if B can be consistently appropriated into A even while it may appear to contradict A.

The first point that must be noted, especially because it is often unnoticed, is that this demand for relevance cannot be the insistence that *values* be consistent with *facts*, but rather that one value or one set of values be made to harmonize with other, competing values. The reason is that facts and values belong to two different categories of existence that are logically independent of each other and therefore cannot stand in a relation of incompatibility. For example, the *fact* that the sun is in the center of the solar system rather than the earth tells us nothing about the relative *value* of the two bodies. The heliocentric hypothesis displaced man from the central position in the universe that he occupied according to the geocentric theory, but this transformation in man's perception of his *position* in the universe has no logical implications for the judgment concerning his *importance* in the scheme of things. The *fact* that the stones and pavements of Jerusalem are composed of chemical elements that may not differ from those in New York, Paris, or London implies nothing whatsoever concerning the sanctity of Jerusalem or the lack of it in another major metropolis.

It is an old philosophical truth, demonstrated once and for all by David Hume, that a value cannot be deduced from a fact, or as he put it, that one cannot infer an "ought" from an "is."[1] Indeed, a central ethical question that moral philosophers have asked in modern times is, What is the place of values in a world of facts? The question is appropriate because the *facts* of the world do not imply *values*, neither ethical nor religious. And if, indeed, there is no logical connection between the two, values cannot be adjusted to conform to facts, and the question of the relevance of one to the other, in the sense of the logical consistency of that which is apparently contradictory, cannot even arise.

The logical independence of values and facts is implicit in a concept of halakhah introduced by Rabbi Joseph B. Soloveitchik. The halakhah, he declared, is a theoretical construction,[2] a value system, derived from an *a priori* source, imposed on the universe of facts.

> Halakhic man, well furnished with rules, judgements, and fundamental principles, draws near the world with an a priori relation. . . . The essence of the Halakhah which he received from God, consists in creating an ideal world and cognizing the relationship between that ideal world and our concrete environment. . . . He desires to coordinate the a priori concepts with the a posteriori phenomenon.[3]

The halakhah does not *discover* but *imposes* sanctity on the Sabbath. When the sun sets on Friday night, there arises, as a result of this imposition, a set of obligations known as the laws of the Sabbath. The halakhah does not reveal but imposes sanctity on the land of Israel. When one lives there, he must assume, because of the halakhic imposition, a set of obligations that comprise "the laws dependent on the land." Facts, whether of a physical or a social nature, do not themselves prescribe values. Moral and religious imperatives do not arise out of the empirical nature of the universe; they are imposed on it. There is no need, therefore, to make the values of Jewish life, as exemplified in mitzvot, relevant to, i.e., consistent, with facts. There is no way in which such values can be incompatible with facts.

The question of relevance can arise only in the relations of *values*, because these often clash. Sometimes the clash takes the form of contradiction. The values of hedonism and narcissism cannot be brought into harmony with those of Judaism, and those of Judaism cannot conform to some of the values embraced by other religions. When in the nineteenth century, synagogues began to mimic patterns of ritual characteristic of other religions, they embraced forms of religious conduct at odds with halakhah. When the American synagogue is turned into a forum of entertainment, as is frequently the case, and in a manner that violates halakhic precepts, values essentially alien to them have invaded the sacred precincts.

Here then is a definition of relevance which makes legitimate the demand that Judaism shall be relevant. There are occasions when the values of Torah appear to confront some competing value which appears to be incompatible with Jewish life but which makes a claim to legitimacy even within the Torah scheme of values. This frequently occurs when the Torah values are compared with those that arise out of the human condition. In such a context, the demand that Judaism should be relevant means that Judaism must somehow take into account and integrate into its value system other values that are essential for human well-being, i.e., that Judaism formulate a relationship between the two that will remove inconsistencies, on the view of *Torah umadda,* or even unite both into a single coherent system of values, according to the perspective of *Torah im derekh eretz.* Good health is necessary for the human organism—it is a basic human value. The question may fairly be put: are the mitzvot of Torah relevant, in the sense here described, to the enterprise of health, i.e., may a person who is ill seek the services of a physician to achieve a cure? It can be argued that Torah and medicine are incompatible because illness is a punishment for sin and the enterprise of healing constitutes defiance of the will of God, in which case Judaism has no relevance to the values embodied in the medical sciences. The question may also be put with respect to the values of science and culture in general. The demand that Judaism should be relevant then means that Judaism shall *not* ignore values of human life and human experience which the Jew ought to appropriate or to which he ought to respond, perhaps even as a matter of religious obligation.

Maimonides speaks of the value of the laws of kashrut. He writes, "I maintain that the food which is forbidden by law is not wholesome. There is nothing among forbidden foods whose injurious character is doubted."[4] Nonkosher foods are therefore, in the Maimonidean view, detrimental to health. Now clearly Maimonides is not saying that the sole purpose of these biblical laws is to ensure human health and well-being. He is not ignoring their spiritual dimension, i.e., the relationship with the Supreme Being that adherence to these laws facilitates. Undoubtedly, for Maimonides, the religious component in the observance of mitzvot is paramount. What he is saying is that the contribution of mitzvot to human well-being must also be acknowledged, i.e., that mitzvot are relevant to values that reflect the human existential condition.

Rabbi Aharon Lichtenstein is the spiritual mentor of a *yeshivat hesder*, a school of Torah study in Israel whose students are required to serve in the Israel Defense Forces. In a rationale of its ideology, he wrote,

> Hesder is not the result of a compromise between the respective positions of *roshei yeshiva* and the Ministry of Defense. . . . We do occasionally argue with the generals over details and they do not always appreciate the preeminence of the spiritual factor. Their basic concern with security, however, is ours no less than theirs.[5]

This is making Judaism relevant. The value inherent in Torah study to which the students in such yeshivot are dedicated must accommodate the human individual and national value of security. The declaration that military service is not a compromise for a Torah student means that service in the military to ensure the security of the state is itself coherent with Torah values. It may even belong in the Torah scheme of things.

The idea of synthesis, promulgated within the halakhic religious community as an ideal worthy of pursuit, is primarily intellectual and academic in character. It requires that students shall engage in the study of science and humanities and simultaneously in the study of Torah. It also has a practical application in that it implies that a Jew shall involve himself in the world of science and technology, in social movements and political actions, even while he is immersed in the study of Torah and in its practice. Now it is important to stress, because this is so frequently misunderstood, that this principle is not a *compromise* but an *ideal*. It does not require that Judaism be adjusted or transformed to fit, to some extent at least, a preconceived alien mold. It does require that Torah values be harmonized with those that emerge out of human and societal conditions, when these are not in direct conflict with halakhic precept, by giving to each due recognition and attention. The *hesder yeshivot*, which respond to the need for national security, and the participation in the Knesset of religiously committed individuals who contribute to the formulation of social policies to ensure the well-being of Israel's citizens are paradigmatic examples of the ideal of synthesis. Security and social welfare are, at the very least, consistent with Torah values. The values of science and the humanities and of culture in general are equally to be accommodated in the Torah perspective. And synthesis is a response to the demands of relevance.

II

The second sense in which the requirement that Judaism be relevant is halakhically legitimate has to do with the enterprise of communicating Torah values. It is obvious that the act of communication involves both a speaker and a listener, and that if a language is unintelligible or even unappealing to the listener, the message will not be successfully transmitted. To be relevant in this sense is to use an idiom that the listener will both understand and appreciate.

Many passages of Maimonides' classic *Guide to the Perplexed* sound strange and incoherent. There are terms such as "potential" and "actual," "form" and "matter," which are assigned a weight that they fail to have for one reared and educated in contemporary scientific terminology. There are assertions, such as the one which claims the identity of the knower, the act of knowing, and the thing known,[6] which are largely incomprehensible even to many among the educated. The reason for this is that the universe of facts and human experience was classified, in the Maimonidean intellectual era, in categories which are not employed today in the textbooks of science. The Maimonidean language which reflects these medieval forms of classification represents a perception and interpretation of the universe that is at present unfamiliar and consequently constitutes a most serious barrier to understanding.

Indeed the language of every generation reveals the mind-set and theoretical perspective of that era and expresses its interpretation of the structure of the world of facts. One who is unfamiliar with its classification will not understand its terminology. For example, one who believes that the essential constituents of material objects are atoms and molecules, electrons and protons, and that the terms referring to these things represent a correct categorization of the elements of nature will not take readily to the claim that the essential components of objects are matter and form, potentiality and actuality, and that the basic elements of things are air, fire, earth, and water. At this juncture, it must be stressed that what Maimonides is saying is not *false* but merely *strange*. He spoke from another perspective, with a different set of theoretical categories and an unfamiliar vocabulary. But if what he was saying, though not false, is strange, it will have little appeal to the philosophically untrained mind.

To be relevant in the communication process, then, is to adopt, not the *propositions* that may be popular in the marketplace of the intellect, not the *doctrines* alien to Judaism by which it is regularly buffeted, but merely the *categories* of language and thought, i.e., the *words* and *concepts* that are useful for the purpose of a modern classification of the facts of human experience. It is to formulate the principles of Jewish life in language that contemporary man will understand. It is not possible to do so without studying the sciences and humanities that are the themes of instruction on the contemporary college campus.

There is a well-known talmudic principle which declares, "The Torah speaks in the language of man."[7] In the context in which it occurs, this statement is interpreted as a literary principle. Rabbi Elazar ben Azariah explained that there are occurrences of words in the Bible which need not be assigned a substantive meaning. They serve a merely literary purpose. For Maimonides, this talmudic assertion means that anthropomorphic expressions, e.g., the hand of God, are utilized when a theologically more accurate formulation would be beyond the intellectual capacity of most people.[8] A third interpretation of this phrase may be offered. The Torah utilizes categories of thought and language which the human being will understand.

Why is the language of Torah called the *lashon hakodesh*, the "holy language"? Nachmanides explains that the holy tongue was originally the Canaanite language,[9] a biblically current mode of discourse. However, he continues in another context, "The reason that our sages called the language of Torah the holy language is that the contents of Torah and the Prophets and everything sacred were said in the holy language."[10] This is the meaning of relevance in the sense of effective communication. It involves utilizing contemporary terminology for the purpose of formulating and articulating the eternal and unchanging principles of Torah.

Notes

Introduction

1. The phrase *Torah umadda* was not used by Rabbi Soloveitchik as nomenclature for his views in *The Lonely Man of Faith*. Nor, to my knowledge, did he ever associate his thought with this phrase. My impression is that he was never too comfortable with labels. Nevertheless, I believe that his distinction between Adam I and Adam II in this work is the most illuminating expression of the *Torah umadda* viewpoint.

Chapter One

1. See Maimonides' commentary on Avot 2:2.

2. Genesis Rabbah 76:3. The phrase *derekh eretz* has the meaning of "acceptable norms of conduct" in many talmudic contexts. See, for example, Bava Metzia 87a and Yoma 4b.

3. Commentary on Genesis 3:24.

4. Makkot 22b.

5. Shabbat 133b.

6. *Iggerot* I, 214.

7. Commentary on Genesis 3:24.

8. Ibid., Genesis 2:7.

9. Hirsch, *The Nineteen Letters of Ben Uziel* (New York: Feldheim, 1960), Letter 16.

10. Commentary on Genesis 1:28.

Chapter Two

1. The difference in meaning between *im* and *u* is described by Rashi in his comment on Ketubbot 8a. The sixth blessing of the *sheva berakhot*, the seven blessings recited at a marriage ceremony, concludes with the phrase "Blessed art Thou, O Lord, who brings joy to the groom and (*u*) the bride." The seventh blessing concludes with the phrase "Blessed art Thou, O Lord, who brings joy to the groom with (*im*) the bride." Rashi explains that the sixth blessing refers to the joy that bride and groom are to experience as

individuals by way of personal achievements and satisfactions even while they are in a married state, while the seventh blessing alludes to the joys that bride together with groom will derive from the marital relationship itself. Thus *im* connotes a unity which is lacking in the meaning of *u*.

2. A unity of combination, accordingly, is suggested by the ideal of *Torah im derekh eretz*.

3. In *The Lonely Man of Faith*, (New York: Doubleday 1992), pp. 12–27.

4. It is necessary to distinguish two meanings of self-assertion. According to one, the self-asserting individual pursues his own interests. He is motivated by egoistic, self-regarding considerations. According to the other, self-assertion manifests itself in egotism, i.e., arrogance. The opposite of egoistic self-assertion is altruism. The opposite of egotistic self-assertion is humility. Only the former is intended in this discussion. See chap. 4 below.

5. See Sol Roth, *The Jewish Idea of Community* (New York: Yeshiva University Press, 1977). In the chapter entitled "The Covenantal Character," a detailed account is given of the difference between covenantal and contractual commitments.

6. *Yalkut Shimoni* (New York: Pardes, 1944), p. 9.

7. Bava Metzia 24b

8. Genesis 33:18.

9. Ibid. 17:1.

10. Luzzatto, *Mesillat Yesharim* (Jerusalem: Eshkol, 1964), p. 127.

11. Op. cit., pp. 12–14.

12. Leviticus 25:10.

13. Nedarim 10a.

14. Op. cit. p. 12.

15. Ibid., p. 78.

16. Ibid., p. 87.

Chapter 3

1. Maimonides, *Mishneh Torah*, Hilkhot Tefillah 1:1.

2. Yoreh De'ah 274:1, 276:2.

3. Shabbat 133b.

4. R. Nissim b. Reuben Gerondi, *Derashot Haran*, ed. Leon Feldman (Jerusalem: Magnes Press, 1974), pp. 191–192.

5. Nachmanides on Deuteronomy 6:18.

6. *Meshekh Ḥokhmah* on Deuteronomy 30:11–14.

7. Hirsch, *Judaism Eternal* (London: Soncino Press, 1956), pp. 174–178.

8. Proverbs 6:6–8.

9. Avot 2:2.

10. *Mishneh Torah*, Hilkhot Melakhim 8:11.

11. Pesaḥim 50b.

Chapter 4

1. Cf. "The Element of Sanctity," in Sol Roth, *The Jewish Idea of Community* (New York: Yeshiva University Press, 1977), pp. 95–100.

2. Shabbat 22b.

3. *Halakhic Man*, trans. Lawrence Kaplan, (Philadelphia: Jewish Publication Society, 1983), p. 40.

4. J. B. Soloveitchik, *The Lonely Man of Faith*, (New York: Doubleday, 1992), p. 35.

5. Ibid., p. 44.

6. Exodus 19:6.

7. Sanhedrin 37a.

8. Ibid.

9. Genesis 18:27

10. Psalms 8:4–6.

11. See the discussion of self-assertion above in chapter 2. There this attitude was endorsed, and here it is rejected. In truth, as indicated in note 4 of above chapter, there are two varieties of self-assertion. One is expressed in egoistic undertakings which are acceptable so long as they do not violate halakhic precepts. The other is manifested in egotism, the posture of superiority in relation to others, which is substantially incompatible with halakhic modalities.

Chapter 5

1. See Bertrand Russell, *The Problems of Philosophy* (New York: Oxford University Press, 1959), chap. 5.

2. J. B. Soloveitchik, *The Halakhic Man*, trans. Lawrence Kaplan (Philadelphia: Jewish Publication Society, 1983), pp. 5–7.

3. Maimonides, *Guide to the Perplexed* (New York: Hebrew Publishing Co.), pt. I, pp. 207–212.

4. Ibid., p. 226.

5. See David Hume, *An Inquiry Concerning Human Understanding* (New York: Library of Liberal Arts, 1955), p. 28.

6. Immanuel Kant, *Prolegomena to Any Future Metaphysics* (New York: Little Library of Liberal Arts, 1950), pp. 60–62.

7. Psalms 118:5.

8. Ibid. 27:4.

9. William James, *Essays in Pragmatism* (New York: Hafner Publishing Co., 1952), p. 106.

10. See Bertrand Russell, "A Free Man's Worship," in his *Mysticism and Logic* (Garden City, N.Y.: Doubleday, 1917); Ernest Nagel, "A Defense of Atheism," in *A New Introduction to Philosophy* ed. S. Cahn (New York: Harper & Row, 1971).

11. Jeremiah 31:15.

12. Jonathan Woocher, "Civil Judaism: The Religion of Jewish Communitas," *Policy Studies '79* (New York: National Jewish Conference Center, 1979), May issue.

Chapter 6

1. Aristotle, *Metaphysics*, bk. I, chap. 1.

2. Aristotle, *Nicomachean Ethics*, bk. X, chap. 7.

3. J. B. Soloveitchik, *The Lonely Man of Faith* (New York: Doubleday: 1992), p. 18.

4. Ibid., pp. 18–19.

5. Avot 3:21.

6. Shabbat 133a.

7. Op cit., p. 43.

8. Commentary on Genesis 3:24.

9. Maimonides, *Mishneh Torah*, Hilkhot Yesodei Hatorah 2:2.

10. J. B. Soloveitchik, *Halakhic Man*, trans. Lawrence Kaplan (Philadelphia: Jewish Publication Society, 1983), p. 7.

11. Mordechai Breuer, "The `Torah-im-Derekh-Eretz' of Samson Raphael Hirsch," *Hama'yon* 9, nos. 1–2 (5729).

12. Commentary on Genesis 9:27.

13. Ibid.

14. *The Nineteen Letters* (New York: Feldheim, 1960), p. 32.

15. Shabbat 133b.

Chapter 7

1. J. B. Soloveitchik, *The Lonely Man of Faith* (New York: Doubleday, 1992), p. 25.

2. Ibid., p. 16.

3. Ibid., p. 17.

4. Shabbat 133b.

5. Op. cit., pp. 16–17.

6. J. S. Mill, *Utilitarianism* (New York: Liberal Arts Press, 1953), p. 9.

7. Psalms 8:6.

8. Commentary on Genesis 1:26.

9. Ibid.

10. Ibid. 1:28.

11. Ibid. 1:26.

12. Soloveitchik, op. cit., p. 36.

13. Ibid., p. 24.

14. Ibid., p. 35.

15. Gershom Scholem, *Major Trends in Jewish Mysticism* (New York: Schocken, 1941), p. 123.

16. Ecclesiastes 3:19.

17. Philip Birnbaum, ed., *High Holiday Prayer Book* (New York: Hebrew Publishing Co.), p. 364.

Chapter 8

1. J. B. Soloveitchik, *Halakhic Man*, trans. Lawrence Kaplan (Philadelphia: Jewish Publication Society, 1983), p. 57.

2. Cf. the discussion of this point in *Biur Hagra*, Oraḥ Ḥayyim 261:1.

3. Proverbs 3:12.

4. Julius Guttmann, *Philosophies of Judaism* (New York: Holt, Rinehart & Winston, 1964), p. 381.

5. Maimonides, *Eight Chapters*, chap. 4.

6. *Sefer Haḥinnukh*, mitzvah 20.

7. *Halakhic Man*, pp. 57–58.

8. S. Roth, *The Jewish Idea of Community* (New York: Yeshiva University Press, 1977), p. 29.

9. Deuteronomy 17:8–12.

10. Nachmanides on Deuteronomy 17:11.

11. Sanhedrin 86b.

12. *Mishneh Torah*, Hilkhot Tefillah 4:15–16.

13. Berakhot 54a.

14. Ibid. 60a.

15. *Mishneh Torah*, Hilkhot Yesodei Hatorah 2:2.

16. J. B. Soloveitchik, *The Lonely Man of Faith* (New York: Doubleday, 1992), p. 2.

Chapter 9

1. Ernest Nagel, *Logic Without Metaphysics* (Glencoe, Ill.: Free Press, 1956), p. 87.

2. Bertrand Russell, *Mysticism and Logic* (Garden City: Doubleday, 1917), p. 150.

3. *Halakhic Man*, trans. Lawrence Kaplan (Philadelphia: Jewish Publication Society, 1983), pp. 18–19.

4. Ibid.

5. Richard R. Braithwaite, *Scientific Explanation* (Cambridge: At the University Press, 1953), p. 91.

6. For an expanded discussion of this point, see Sec. I of Ch. 14.

7. *Kitvei Ramban* (Jerusalem: Mosad Harav Kook, 1963), p. 374.

Chapter 10

1. Plato, *Phaedo*, in *The Dialogues of Plato*, ed. B. Jowett (New York: Random House, 1937), vol. 2, p. 447.

2. Midrash Genesis Rabbah 9:9; also cited in chap. 2 above.

3. J.T. Ta'anit 4:4.

4. Maimonides, *Mishneh Torah*, Hilkhot Teshuvah 3:7.

5. J. B. Soloveitchik, *Halachic Man*, trans. Lawrence Kaplan (Philadelphia: Jewish Publication Society, 1983) p. 40

6. S. R. Hirsch, *Horeb*, trans. I. Grunfeld (London: Soncino Press, 1962), vol. 1, p. 11..

7. Rashi on Genesis 6:13.

8. Maimonides, *Mishneh Torah*, Hilkhot Melakhim 12:1.

9. Sanhedrin 71a, referring to the law in Deuteronomy 21:18–21.

10. This principle is enunciated in a variety of ways in halakhic discussions; e.g., the declaration in Shabbat 76a to the effect that if something is difficult to eat, the act of consuming it cannot be designated "eating."

11. Betzah 15b, Pesaḥim 68b.

12. Maimonides, *Mishneh Torah*, Hilkhot Yom Tov 6:19–20.

13. Rashi on Pesaḥim 68b.

14. Isaiah 58:13.

15. See also Sol Roth, *Halakhah and Politics: The Jewish Idea of a State* (New York: Yeshiva University Press, 1988), p. 31.

Chapter 11

1. Cf. above, chap. 1.

2. Deuteronomy 17:19.

3. Sotah 41a.

4. See the discussion of this point in chap. 1 above.

5. The performance of a mitzvah requires an awareness that what one is doing constitutes a response to a divine command. Even the view which maintains that a mitzvah can be fulfilled without *kavvanah* grants that, in the ideal form, the awareness of the Divine Being as the source of the obligation is desirable. This is not essential, according to Rabbi Soloveitchik, in fulfilling the mandate of *vekhivshuha*. One who is engaged in that enterprise belongs to the community of interest, in which God is not present. See the discussion of this point in chap. 6.

6. Sanhedrin 20b. Note too that Maimonides, in *Mishneh Torah*, Hilkhot Melakhim 1:1, regarded it as a mitzvah, an obligation to apply the law of the king, whereas Abarbanel, in his commentary on Deuteronomy 17, adopts a position similar to that of Rav, merely tolerating the institution of a sovereign.

7. The Torah prescribes two varieties of mitzvah. One is categorical, i.e., a mitzvah whose performance is required irrespective of any circumstances that may arise (so long as one is capable of performing it, and when it is not set aside because it is incompatible with another mitzvah which, for one reason or another, is assigned priority); e.g., the obligation to recite the Shema or to eat matzah on Passover. The other variety is conditional, i.e., a mitzvah whose fulfillment depends on certain conditions being present; e.g., one is obligated to build a fence around the roof of one's house, but need not buy a house to fulfill this mitzvah. Whether the mitzvah to designate a sovereign is categorical or hypothetical is the subject of talmudic debate. In either case, however, it is a mitzvah.

8. Genesis 15:18.

9. See above, chap. 10.

10. Sanhedrin 20b.

11. Judges 5:16.

12. Maimonides, *Mishneh Torah*, Hilkhot Melakhim 1:3.

13. A. I. Kook, *Mishpat Kohen* (Jerusalem, 1937), p. 337.

Chapter 12

1. Genesis 6:13.

2. Cf. *Fear and Trembling* by Soren Kierkegaard, who argues that the knight of faith is always ready to do God's bidding even if the act required is, to normal perception, simply murder. On his interpretation of the binding of Isaac, when God demands a response, even if its purpose is merely a *test* of faith, all ethical considerations become irrelevant.

3. Isaiah 55:6. Some argue that the Bible perceives the divine and human concepts of justice as identical. They offer as evidence the argument presented by Abraham in behalf of the people of Sodom, "The Judge of the entire earth will not do justice?" (Genesis 18:25). This question could not have been asked unless it was assumed that divine and human share the same concept of justice. It should be noted, however, that God, in response to Abraham, did not admit that He was in error and that His original intention had indeed been unjust. Rather, He changed His decision in order to accommodate Abraham, whom He loved because "he commands his children and his household to follow the ways of God and to behave with righteousness and justice in the land" (Genesis 18:19). God merely moved from the principle of justice to that of mercy.

4. Psalms 145:19.

5. See the discussion of this principle and the biblical basis for it in Sanhedrin 79a.

6. Cf. Maimonides, *Mishneh Torah*, Hilkhot Edut 18:2–3. See also Bava Kamma 72b, in which it is declared that the law of falsification is a novelty because two witnesses are opposed by an equal number in the case of both contradiction and falsification; why then should the second pair have more credibility in one case than in the other? This is clearly a nonrational component in the talmudic concept of justice.

7. Cf R. Nissim b. Reuben Gerondi, *Derashot Haran*, ed. Leon A. Feldman (Jerusalem: Magnes Press, 1974), pp. 191–192.

8. This distinction also lies at the basis of the exposition of the *ta'amei hamitzvot*, "reasons for the commandments," by many classic commentators of the Bible. The very attempt to suggest such reasons presupposes that whatever transcendental factors may have been involved in the divine decision to choose these as the rules of human conduct, there was in addition a human element. The commandments may be viewed from the perspective of God or from that of man, and the two need not be identical. We can form no conception of how we might justify Torah precepts from the point of view of the Transcendent Being. From the human perspective, they have in fact been interpreted in terms of the needs of the individual or the exigencies of society. The implication, according to those who undertake to give an account of the reasons for the commandments, is that their rationale is two-dimensional, i.e., they express the Divine Will and are responsive to human needs. Obviously, human factors do provide the basis for Torah legislation.

9. Cf. Aharon Lichtenstein, "Does Jewish Tradition Recognize an Ethic Independent of Halakha?" in *Contemporary Jewish Ethics*, ed. M. M. Kellner (New York: Sanhedrin Press, 1978).

10. Rashi on Genesis 1:1.

11. Deuteronomy 13:9.

12. Numbers 35:24–25.

13. In *Pesikta d'Rav Kahana*, cited in S. Y. Agnon, *Yamim Nora'im* (Jerusalem: Schocken Press, 1946), p. 97.

14. Maimonides, *Mishneh Torah*, Hilkhot Teshuvah 2:6.

15. Ibid. 1:4.

16. Sanhedrin 27b.

17. Kohelet Rabbah 7:36.

18. Zechariah 8:16.

19. Sanhedrin 6b.

20. Ḥoshen Mishpat 12:2.

21. This is not to be taken to mean that peace is perceived to be of greater importance than justice in the rabbinic perspective. Peace of a lasting nature cannot be based on injustice. It is rather the case that there are two varieties of justice—that which requires strict application of the law, i.e., adjudication, and that which includes a component of compromise and generosity, i.e. arbitration. For a full discussion of this point, see the chapter entitled "Peace" in S. Roth, *Halakhah and Politics: The Jewish Idea of a State* (New York: Ktav, 1988), pp. 142.–151.

Chapter 13

1. Genesis 25:23.

2. Isaiah 2:3.

3. Genesis 15:13–16.

4. Deuteronomy 4:25–30, 32:7–43.

5. Rashi on Genesis 33:4.

6. Nachmanides on Genesis 12:6.

7. Megillah 6a.

8. Isaiah 60:22.

9. Sanhedrin 98a.

10. It is true that many who are not biologically descended from the patriarchs were included in the Jewish community as a result of the process of conversion. Yet following admission to Jewish life, birth still figures as the basis for identification. The offspring of the convert is Jewish because

he was born into a Jewish family. Family relationship remains the essential feature of membership.

11.Thomas Hobbes, *Leviathan*, in *The English Philosophers from Bacon to Mill* (New York: Modern Library, 1939), p. 160.

12. The two varieties of hatred are described in S. Roth, "Black Anti-Semitism: Diagnosis and Treatment," *Judaism* 30 (Summer 1981).

13. E.g., see Leviticus 36:26–43 and Deuteronomy 28:15–68.

14. The Musaf service of the major festivals.

15. Deuteronomy 8:5.

16. Ibid., v. 3.

17. Berakhot 5a.

18. Proverbs 3:12.

19. Berakhot 7a.

20. Rashi on ibid. 5a.

21. Rashi on Genesis 6:13.

22. Maimonides, *Mishneh Torah*, Hilkhot Melakhim 12.

23. What follows in this chapter should be read in conjunction with section 4 of chapter 5, which also elaborates on the concept of Jewish destiny. Some repetition is inevitable.

24. Musaf Amidah.

Chapter 14

1. Hume, *A Treatise of Human Nature* (Oxford: Clarendon Press, 1955), p. 469.

2. Chapter 9 in this volume is devoted to an analysis of the concept of halakhah as a theoretical construction.

3. J. B. Soloveitchik, *Halakhic Man* (Philadelphia: Jewish Publication Society, 1983), pp. 19–20.

4. Maimonides, *Guide to the Perplexed*, trans. M. Friedländer (New York: Hebrew Publishing Co., 19??), pt. III, p. 251.

5. From *The Ideology of the Hesder, Tradition*, Fall 1991, Vol. 19, pp. 199–217.

6. *Guide to the Perplexed*, pp. 252–259.

7. Kiddushin 17b.

8. *Guide of the Perplexed*, pp. 89–92.

9. Nachmanides on Genesis 45:12.

10. Commentary on Exodus 30:13.

Glossary

avodah spiritual service, originally referring to the divine service in the Temple; see next entry.

avodah shebalev the service of the heart, that is, prayer.

bizui mitzvah an act which leads to disrespect for a mitzvah, as in the denigrating use of an object with whose help a mitzvah was performed.

derekh eretz literally, "the way of the earth." It may mean 'respect', or even 'labor', but in this volume it is used to mean 'culture'.

gavra rabba a great man, usually, a leading Torah scholar

halakhah the biblical and rabbinic code that formulates the precepts of Jewish conduct.

Hesder yeshivot schools of Torah study in Israel whose students serve in the Israel Defense Forces several months of the year.

hester Panim the hiding of [God's] Face, that is, the theological doctrine that when the people of Israel suffers catastrophe, it is often due to the fact that they are withdrawn from God's care.

kashrut the Jewish dietary laws.

kodeish holy.

lifnim mishurat hadin going beyond the letter of the law, often to adhere to a higher standard of ethical sensitivity.

madda knowledge, often used of scientific knowledge gained by means of the application of human reason rather than divine revelation.

melakhah work, usually of the creative variety, especially as regarding the Sabbath laws.

melekh elyon the King Above, that is the Divine Sovereign.

mishpat civil and criminal law.

heftzah shel mitzvah an object with which a mitzvah is performed

hesed lovingkindness.

hetzia lashem vehetzia lekhem literally, "half for God and half for you," that is, the principle that the observance of the festivals requires that a portion of time should be devoted to God in the form of study and prayer and another portion to the consumption of food and drink.

hok a religious law at which a human being could not have arrived on the basis of rational considerations alone

hol secular.

hovat gavra an obligation imposed on a human being.

hovat heftziah an obligation based on the status of an object.

na'ase adam bezalmeinu a biblical phrase which means "Let us make man in our image" (Gen. 1:26).

shelo lishma not for the sake of the mitzvah as, for example, to study Torah for ulterior motives.

sheva berakhot "Seven Blessings," that is, those blessings recited at a wedding ceremony.

shofet a judge.

sukkah a booth erected for the purpose of celebrating the festival of Sukkot (Tabernacles).

tallit a prayer shawl.

tamei something or someone who is spiritually impure.

tefillin phylacteries worn during daily morning prayers.

toeivah an abomination.

Torah im derekh eretz a phrase in the Mishna interpreted by Samson R. Hirsch to mean the need to combine Torah and culture in the religious life of the Jew.

Torah im madda a perspective in which general knowledge is perceived to be included under the rubric of Torah.

Torah umadda a doctrine which declares the legitimacy of studying both Torah and general knowledge without regarding the latter as included in the former.

vekarata lashabbat oneg a phrase which means "thou shalt call the Sabbath a delight" (Isaiah 58:13).

vekhivshuha a biblical term which means "you shall conquer it" (Gen. 1:28), used in halakhic literature to designate humankind's role of bending nature to human ends.

Index